T'ai Chi for Two

T'ai Chi for Two

The Practice of Push Hands

Paul Crompton

 Shambhala

Boston & Shaftesbury

1989

Shambhala Publications, Inc.
Horticultural Hall
300 Massachusetts Avenue
Boston, Massachusetts 02115

Shambhala Publications, Inc.
The Old School House
The Courtyard, Bell Street
Shaftesbury, Dorset SP7 8BP

9 8 7 6 5 4 3 2 1

First Edition

Printed in the United States of America

Distributed in the United States by Random House
and in Canada by Random House of Canada Ltd.
Distributed in the United Kingdom by Element Books Ltd.
Photographs by Louanne Richards

Crompton, Paul H., 1936–
  T'ai chi for two : the practice of push hands / Paul Crompton — 1st ed.
    p.   cm.
  Bibliography: p.
  Includes index.
  ISBN 0-87773-468-2
  1. T'ai chi ch'üan. I. Title.
GV504.C77 1989   88-34335
796.8'155—dc19   CIP

Contents

1. Exercise for Two / 1

2. Who Is Your Partner? / 5

3. The Concept of *Ch'i* / 12

4. Some Personal Experiences / 19

5. Stories and Sayings / 26

6. Empty Mind / 33

7. Push Hands Training / 37

8. More Push Hands / 51

9. Brawn . . . but Brains / 84

10. The Shape of the Movement / 92

11. Taoism and T'ai Chi Ch'uan / 104

Conclusion / 117

Some Taoist Terms / 118

Bibliography / 121

1   *Exercise for Two*

T'ai Chi Ch'uan is best known as a slow, gentle exercise performed alone, and in fact the sequence of movements involved is commonly called the Solo Form to indicate this. But there is another important side to T'ai Chi, called Pushing Hands or Push Hands, that is less well known. Push Hands is done with a partner, and visually it is not as beautiful or interesting as the Solo Form, which may explain why it has received so little publicity. All the elements of the Solo Form—including relaxation, flow, nonresistance or yielding, and the use of the body as a whole unit—enter into Push Hands. Because you are touching and being touched by another person, all these elements are difficult to maintain. This is one's first impression. But with time you become able to include your partner in your activity, almost as if he or she were a part of yourself, and then these difficulties diminish. Of course, other difficulties arise, as they do in any worthwhile activity, and I will be discussing these later in this book.

When I was introduced to Push Hands methods in about 1968 with my first teacher, I spent very little time on them, as I was learning the Solo Form. It is not usual or necessary to learn Push Hands first, although it can be learned at the same time as the Solo Form. It was some years later that I came back to Push Hands with another teacher. In the early years I did not see the potential usefulness of the two-person discipline. Proficiency in the Form is one level of attainment, but proficiency in Push Hands is on a higher level. This will become clearer as we move along.

The basic principle of Push Hands is yielding. If someone pushes me, I do not resist but give way while not losing contact. This principle is often cited in connection with the Japanese art of Judo, but in Judo it has virtually disappeared, as any five-second viewing of a Judo tournament will confirm. It makes its appearance in some forms of Aikido also, but the Aikido I have seen and done myself has it only to a very limited degree. The reason for the scarcity of skill in Push Hands is that it requires a change in the character of the student himself. If you say to someone, "When I push you, do not resist me but give way," then at the first attempt your partner will perhaps succeed. He or she will be less successful the second time and will actually resist you the third time. Your partner's awareness of what he or she is doing is so weak, and the in-built tendency to meet force with force is so strong, that your request to yield disappears from the other's mind very quickly.

This is why I feel that a book such as this one is a positive contribution to our lives as well as to an understanding of the subject itself. If we can learn something, even a little, about our reactions to other people, and begin to cope with them, then our time will not have been wasted. Other books on Push Hands are available, but they take so much for granted that they fail, in my opinion, to lay a solid foundation on which to build. In such a study as T'ai Chi you cannot take anything for granted.

Who can make muddy water clear? This question of the Chinese sages we can try to answer. We can run clear water through muddy water time and again by right training. We can let the muddy particles settle by deep relaxation. We can simply throw it away, by trying to grapple with our habits and explore the marvelous adaptability and versatility of the body. If you follow the suggestions in this book with a partner, you will reach some degree of skill in Push Hands. I sincerely hope it will be of some value to you in the difficult times in which we live. I should add that everything given in this book has been tried and pursued by me and my students countless times. It is practical.

Books that tell you how to do something naturally say, "Do this, then do that." There is an underlying assumption that you *can* do this and that. Or the hope is implied that sooner or later you will be able to. But as anyone who has ever bought such a book will tell you, these assumptions and hopes do not always bear fruit. A friend of mine who is a business consultant and computer wizard told me once that in business over fifty percent of all processes have to be done over to get them right. More time and money are spent in correcting errors than in producing the desired result. He cited companies that have done research on this problem and are trying to put it right.

Can an individual perform better than a company? Maybe you can find out for yourself in connection with Push Hands. A useful thing to remember in this endeavor is to aim to do one thing at a time. This is very difficult. We can take an example. I ask you to stand up and you do it right now. That is one thing. Then I ask you to stand with your feet shoulder-width apart. That's another thing. Then turn the toe of you left foot out at a forty-five degree angle to the direction in which you are facing. Step directly forward about fifteen inches with your right foot, your toes pointing dead ahead. Then do the same stepping forward with the left foot. Now check your position. Are you leaning forward a little towards your front foot? If so, then you have failed, because you added something of your own to what was asked. This trivial exercise illustrates the point about getting things right the first time. It also shows something about doing one thing at a time. This standing position is basic to Push Hands, as you will see later in the photographs, so it is essential to learn it first. Try to get each instruction right the first time, with an attitude of "make haste slowly."

Obviously you need a partner to study Push Hands. You might invite a friend or your husband or wife to practice with you. If no one is willing, then join a T'ai Chi class. As the methods I am giving here may not be exactly the same as in all other classes, you may have to persuade another class member to train with you outside the school if you want to pursue them. I mention this because unfortunately some teachers are surprisingly unwilling to allow their pupils to do anything that does not conform to the studio syllabus. You need someone who is open to experimenting, someone who is not fixed on the idea of "winning" and who is prepared to accept Push Hands as a psychological experiment as much as a physical one. You will not develop big muscles from this art, but your stretchability in the legs, waist, and lower abdomen will improve remarkably with time. In the beginning your thigh muscles may ache, but this will pass off.

I have covered the basics of T'ai Chi practice in my previous book, *The T'ai Chi Workbook* (published in the United Kingdom as *Chinese Soft Exercise*), and in this second volume I assume that you already have some knowledge of loosening and relaxing. The layout here is necessarily different, but I am writing in the same style, trying to be as simple as I can. This is not because I regard readers as simpletons but because I have found that in teaching T'ai Chi it is necessary, again and again, to open even the apparently obvious to examination. Do not think as you read and look that a movement that looks easy is easy. As you will discover, it is not the outside of Push Hands that is important but rather how you are inside. So sometimes the easiest-looking movement can be the most difficult. With experience this is seen to be true. That is probably why to an outsider the conversation of any insiders is incomprehensible and boring.

Try to bear in mind that your training partner is a human being just like you, not the enemy or an obstacle to overcome. Your partner has thoughts and feelings, muscles and organs, strengths and weaknesses, just like you. Push Hands should be done with humanity. It is like being a good gardener or a kind and affectionate lover. The desire to "win" is like a disease that penetrates into the action itself, into the muscles, and cuts off sensitivity and watchfulness.

2 *Who Is Your Partner?*

Someone once told me that there is a tribe in Mongolia with an interesting trait. When they meet someone, these people never smile. They simply look very directly at him, with openness, taking him in. They see him, his dress, his face, how he moves, and so forth. In our society we would probably find this strange, even rude and hostile. It is the accepted norm with us to smile, shake hands perhaps, make inconsequential remarks about the weather, and hide behind a welter of social platitudes, be they verbal or physical. Unlike the Mongolian tribespeople, we wish neither to see nor to be seen.

On the physical level our gestures and postures during this social game are awkward and tense. When these gestures and postures are measured scientifically, the muscular action appears on a printout as jagged, leaping lines and sporadic bursts of movement showing an underlying unease and lack of good muscle tone. We are blocking our channels of communication between one another, though on the surface it looks as if we are doing quite the opposite. The reasons for this behavior are not the topic of this book, but the observed facts are important to bear in mind when exploring the subject of Push Hands. This is because one of the possible results of training is to release us for a time from patterns of tension. To be released from something, it is necessary to know that we are caught by it. G. I. Gurdjieff said that we are all in prison but that before we can wish to escape from prison, we must first of all realize that we are there. If we think we are free, why should we try to escape?

One of the keys to our prison is to discover something about being more *related*. How is the body to become more related to the mind? In the social scene described above, the tensions are preventing any of this kind of relationship from taking place. In Push Hands training we are taking a further step in pursuit of relationship because we need to discover how to relate to another person—the partner. So who is the partner? The discovery is twofold because in getting to know myself better I get to know the other better. "Who is my neighbor?" asked the lawyer of Jesus. On a more lowly level we can ask this question about our partner.

Push Hands is an excellent acid test of how well I am related because it uses the body, and for most intents and purposes the body cannot lie. I can lie to myself and say that I am not tense, that I do not feel antagonism towards my partner, and that I do not care if I am given a push. But if, when pushed, I become tense and resentful and so lose my balance, this cannot be hidden. It is plainly felt by me and seen and experienced by my partner. It shows in my posture because my body loses its unity. When I stand in the correct posture for Push Hands, with my trunk erect, my knees bent, elbows down, and looking horizontally, my body and to some extent my mind are more related. But when my partner pushes me and an emotional reaction of antagonism or fear arises, my posture loses its cohesiveness and the relationship is broken. In most of the ancient Ways (Tao) that we know about—from whatever country they came—the body plays an important and graphic role. The Ways of the brush, the sword, tea, archery, and unarmed combat associated with Zen are widely known. The postures of Yoga and the lovely classical dances of India are further examples. The turning of the Muslim dervishes of the Middle East is central to their Way, in at least one school, and the ritual gestures, or *mudra*, of Tibet appear in many examples of Tibetan art. It is said that Jesus and his disciples used to dance. This all indicates that in pursuing our theme of *relationship* we are on the right track.

Your Partner Is Your Mirror

The image of the mirror or the still, mirrorlike surface of water is one that often appears in sayings and stories of the Ways. When a mirror is unclouded and the surface of water is still, it gives a true and clear reflection of what is before it. We can learn something from this image because people who have studied Push Hands in some detail and with a degree of impartiality have found that the partner is very much a true reflection of oneself. We all secretly believe, perhaps with some justification, that we are unique and special. But if we are, it is not in the field of our usual interpersonal relationships. This is regularly and humorously illustrated in the endless diet of situation comedies that feed television audiences. We all laugh so readily at them because we see ourselves there on the screen—flirting with the neighbor's wife, fiddling our expenses, struggling to pass the driving test, and fuming in traffic jams. Likewise, when I put my hands on my partner's arm in Push Hands and give a push and when I sense his or her body beginning to tense and feel an antagonistic reaction to me, I can be sure that when that person pushes me I am just the same. This raises a further question: In view of the fact that my partner is just like me and that I am just like my partner, what is my attitude towards him or her? Can it be modified, even for a while?

When you walk into a class where Push Hands is being taught, you immediately become prey to your reactions. All around you are people of difference race, class, build, education, dress, mannerisms, and so on. Faced by a heavily built, dark, menacing-looking man, you will react differently from the way you would react to a willowy, blue-eyed blond woman. It is obvious on the cold, printed page but perhaps not readily observed in oneself in the class. But behind the physical forms of the two people used as examples there lie the same emotional reactions, more or less, that you experience in yourself; fear and antagonism. The dark, heavily built man, for all his appearance, is still worried about being pushed, especially by someone weaker and smaller. And the blond woman does not want her poise and charm to be upset in spite of the fact that she realizes that she is possibly the weakest person in the class. They are both protecting something, even though there is virtually no danger of physical injury.

In Push Hands training we begin to gnaw away at the bars of our emotional prison in three ways. We train the body to begin to move in a different way; we train the mind to be on the alert and watch over the body and its movements; and we try to encourage our emotions to be more open to other people. Gurdjieff referred to these three parts of ourselves as centers, or brains. He said that in general the three centers of intellect, body, and emotion work in isolation from one another. They are not related, and what is needed is for human beings to begin to study how to bring these three brains into relationship with one another. Push Hands, as a vestige of ancient Taoist teaching, points in the same direction. But Push Hands today all too often lacks the knowledge and understanding that the heirs of Gurdjieff's transmission possess. Having said that, one should not conclude that Push Hands merely scratches the surface. One can study it for a lifetime and still have more to learn from it.

Standing there in the class with the hands of the dark, heavily built man resting on your elbow and wrist, how do you feel? What are you doing? Is he going to push you so hard that you fly out of the window? Of course not. You know he is not going to do that, but inside you are feeling as though he might. Your body becomes tense in order to stop him from pushing you. What is he thinking and feeling? Is he looking down on you like some insect that he will brush aside? Perhaps. Perhaps not. There is only one point that need concern you. The only contact between him and you is where he touches you. Everything else is imagination. This is so even if he is as strong as Goliath. Your brain, or intellect, comes into play here. Your job right now is to remember this. It brings to mind a T'ai Chi saying to the effect that a force of four ounces can deflect a force of a thousand pounds—if it is applied correctly.

As we study the changing of pushing straight lines into curves, we begin to see that aggression is an enemy of intelligence. The act of moving into a curve requires intelligence. The straight-line resistance needs none. So at all times you are looking for the curve. It is worthwhile here to refer to a key diagram, that of Yin and Yang (Figure 1). This symbol is well known, but it is not time wasted to go over it again. The two "fishes" represent two of the three forces that are said to support the whole of creation. The white fish is Yang, positive, with a black (Yin) eye. The black fish is Yin, negative, with a white (Yang) eye. At the extreme end of the white fish there is a minimum of negative force. At the head there is maximum. Where there is maximum Yin there is minimum Yang, but potentially there is maximum Yang too. It depends on which moment you choose to compare. It is always changing. Across the middle of both fish there is an equilibrium of forces. The eyes of both fish are a reminder that for us there is no absolute Yin or Yang; each contains something from the other.

In Push Hands we think of pushing as Yang, yielding as Yin. Yin reduces the power of Yang just as a woman first arouses and then reduces the passion of a man. The idea of Yin and Yang and their relationship, making three forces in all, is a beautiful and life-giving one. With its help we can try to understand Push Hands in action and at the same time our relationship with our partner.

Faced with the dark, heavily built man, you can see him not in the form of a threatening superior force but as a carrier of the forces of Yin and Yang. When he pushes I experience the Yang force and try to find the Yin force in myself. My joints and muscles give way under the influence of this idea, and I neutralize his force by leading him into a

Figure 1

curve. His Yang force travels from the head of the fish down to the tail, diminishing. My Yin force increases in proportion, but in doing so my potential Yang force increases too. His actual Yang force diminishes, but his potential Yin force increases. When I turn his arms, ready to push him, for an almost imperceptible moment the two forces are in equilibrium. Then my Yang push begins to send him back, and he meets it with Yin. So the cycle continues; not a struggle between fears and antagonism but a balancing of Yin and Yang forces, experienced in the body and watched over by the mind.

We must not forget the eyes of the two fishes. When you are pushing, or Yang, you keep a taste of yielding in your muscles, to avoid impetuousness. When you yield, or become Yin, you keep a flavor of Yang, otherwise your partner would have nothing to push against at all.

In such an enterprise as Push Hands we should distinguish between aims and possibilities. It is our aim to let the principles of Push Hands fill us completely for a while. But our present possibility of doing so is small. It does not matter, though. Like the mouse who tried to go to Mecca, we are on our way. We noted earlier that the important points of contact with a partner are initially the wrist and elbow. We can remember that it is not just the wrist and elbow that must yield; it is the whole body. When my partner pushes my arm, I must try to experience it right down to the soles of my feet. If I do this, then my whole body moves as a unit, not in separate pieces. This is difficult at the beginning because of my emotional reactions. When I am afraid or worried, one or two parts of my body become tenser than others. I become easy to push over. Similarly, my partner pushes and my arm is carried back in contact with my body, it seems as though there is nowhere else to yield. It is at this type of juncture that we need some agreement beforehand. If my partner continues to push, I will go off balance. So he or she gives me a chance and lets me find another direction to yield in, maybe by turning the body itself to left or right. The partner does not give way to a wish to win, and I have an opportunity to find a way out. Searching rapidly through my sensations of balance and posture, I find another direction and yield in it.

This is a most important moment in Push Hands training. It is relatively easy to learn to give way in one direction. After a time a beginner can do it automatically. But when a new situation arises such as having an arm pushed against the body, it is a new experience. Usually in this situation the beginner freezes, and everything learned so far goes out the window. He or she is back at square one. This "second stage" needs to be studied. It has countless parallels in daily life, of course. As this is an introductory book and the reader probably has little or no Push Hands experience, it would not be constructive to go into this second stage in detail, since most of what might be said would be too theoretical. Definitions of experience would have to be established in detail also. But if you analyze for yourself what happens and follow the Yin-Yang principle, you will begin to find your own way.

Remember that softness is not flabbiness. Cheng Man-Ch'ing said that he never allowed anyone to put more that a few ounces of pressure on him. But we cannot begin there. Our initial efforts have to be much coarser before we can move on to such fine experiences. Gradually, as we continue to explore Push Hands, we find more and more subtlety. We go past the initial stage into a world of subterfuge. If my partner pushes me softly, I offer more hardness to push on. This draws the Yang out of him and gives me more to go on. But it also decreases my position since the other in turn can detect my balance more easily. At this moment I must step up my awareness of what is taking place. Remember that although Push Hands is performed slowly at first, a whole round of push, yield, push, yield only takes seconds. This clear increase in the complexity need not daunt us. It simply raises the perennial question of spontaneity and technique. We need both. As someone once said to me, "Prepare what you have to say and be ready to improvize." We learn more and more Push Hands techniques until, like the Zen master who deflected a sword with a chopstick, we act without knowing technique. We follow, like a rider following the movements of a horse.

A useful practical point for your partner and you to remember is the following: sometimes, when you are pushing, stop moving. If your partner continues to move back, you know that he or she is just moving mechanically, not sensing your movement. This is a good test of attention. This sensing of pressure, rising and falling, is half of the Push Hands training. The other half is knowing what to do about it.

So who is my partner? My partner is the person who is going to teach me through simply being there. Without my partner I can get nowhere, so I can be a little grateful. My partner can show me that fear and antagonism, resentment and ambition are undesirable—not because the Sunday school teacher says so but because they cut me off from myself and from the other person. What is necessary, as the story about the Mongolians showed, is for us to be open to the person in front to us—to what is—and not prey to an image that we think we must at all costs preserve. This is a big thing.

3   *The Concept of Ch'i*

In my first book I touched on the subject of *ch'i*. Since then, interest in the subject has grown, and articles in magazines and new books have helped to swell that interest. Therefore, it is useful to say more about it.

Chapter 11 goes into more detail about *ch'i* and Taoism from the orthodox point of view. Here I would like to look at it in a different way. *Ch'i*, or vitality, is a concept that has disappeared from our current ideas in the West. It has no place in our pragmatic scientific outlook or in our theories about art, physical education, dance, or sport. But at the time of Anton Mesmer (1733–1815), the man who gave his name to the terms *mesmerism* and *mesmerize,* such a concept was current. Mesmerism later became more widely known as hypnotism. Expressions like *animal magnetism*, *universal fluids*, *bodily stroking,* and similar phrases appeared in journals and other publications. Mesmer was a sincere seeker after medical knowledge, but his contemporaries pilloried him, and his search was diverted. Just before the Russian Revolution the notorious monk Rasputin was reputed to have miraculous healing energy, the use of which helped to cure the Czar's son. When he had used some of this energy, the story goes, he was exhausted. Healers speak of "making passes" over the bodies of their patients, to recharge and change the energy flow. When I was a youngster I read about a clergyman who, after a lifetime of seeking healing power, began to cure people through the laying on of hands, and he experienced a powerful flow of heat in his hands. All these people, having different backgrounds of ideas, described invisible energy in different ways. So, although in the West we have no single concept running through all levels of society, we do have a widespread belief in invisible energy. This lack of a single concept distinguishes us very markedly from the Chinese, who have the single concept *ch'i*.

In Chinese art, martial arts, craftsmanship, and drama there is obviously a physical form—and it is readily assessed—but these activities are also qualified by the degree of *ch'i* emitted or present. A spectator might say that a series of movements was correct but that the level of *ch'i* was low. It lacked the right energy; it lacked life. A Chinese traditional doctor will take the pulses and observe whether the *ch'i* in the body is Yin or Yang. People who go deeply into the study of T'ai Chi aim to accumulate *ch'i* in the body.

As I have written a lot about martial arts, especially T'ai Chi, I feel it is my responsibility to say something about "*ch'i* power," a term used often in such circles. I feel this particularly strongly because the people who are most commonly attracted to it are the young and impressionable and people genuinely in need of some guidance in their lives. All too often *ch'i* power is presented as some kind of magic pill that will change everything or as a means of gaining instant mastery of opponents in combat. Therefore my position has to be a critical one, and I hope I will not be condemned for it. There are plenty of people who take a promotional position, to counterbalance my few words.

Beginning with the coarsest and most obvious arguments, take a look at sports and warfare. If the attainment of *ch'i* power were so easy and within everyone's grasp, where are the athletes and soldiers to prove it? If the advocates of *ch'i* power were correct in their assumption, we would expect the Eastern nations to make use of the traditional techniques. The contrary in fact is true: Eastern countries mainly rely on Western systems of training for both their athletes and their soldiers. When a friend of mine who was studying at a Kung Fu school in Taiwan went to the master with a headache, he was handed a bottle of aspirin, not cured with *ch'i* power. Yet we commonly find *ch'i* put forward as a remedy for hypertension, neuroses, chronic insomnia, and a host of other ailments. Here too we have to admit a gross exaggeration of the facts. Finally, we have the use of *ch'i* control to reach enlightenment as advertised in dozens of books. The feasibility of this is not at issue here. What is at issue is that if such a course were as easy and straightforward as the books make it seem, there would be hundreds of thousands of enlightened people in the world. When we see the state of our world as reported by the newspapers and television, we must sadly conclude that this is not true.

It was made clear to me some thirty-three years ago that *ch'i* power and all similar concepts should be looked at in a particular way. When we hear about a system or method, we are conditioned by our education and society to think of it as a course, like learning how to drive a car. We approach it in the spirit of absorbing it into our way of life, as if, in some sense, it were smaller than we are. The opposite is true.

Ch'i is such a profound subject and reaches so far into us that we ought to see that we are almost too small to approach it. Expressions like "tap into the power of the universe" demonstrate a lack of respect and understanding and a failure of conscience about other people. How could anyone who genuinely cares about others promise them that they can control the *ch'i*? The *ch'i* controls us, and we should be grateful for that. If we had to bear the responsibility of controlling it, we would be dead in five seconds.

One of the most written-about and powerful aspects of *ch'i* is related to the sexual region of the body. It is said that one can control this intrinsic sexual energy, lead it up to a specific part of the body, and concentrate it there. Whatever Taoist masters could and can do, and whether the traditional texts contain full descriptions of these practices, is not important here. What is important is a simple question: If an attractive male or female passes your field of vision, do you notice? The answer is yes. You notice, you watch, and you continue to watch until he or she disappears round the corner. It is the same with all sexual experiences. Sexual energy moves at a speed and with a compelling power that is amazing. Every normal and healthy person is driven by sexual energy at more or less frequent intervals. We don't need to dwell on that, it is so clear. Any unusual interference with the sexual instinct leads to mental and physical problems. So many researchers have gone into the subject that one can go into any bookshop and immediately find a copy of Dr. So-and-So's latest findings on the sexual problems of such-and-such a group in society. We then turn around from these observations of daily life and find that someone has written a book, or is teaching a course, all about harnessing sexual energy by the use of *ch'i*. To follow such practices is, in my opinion, a mistake. To read about them and understand the theory is another matter. But it is best to be cautious about publications that promote science-fiction-like notions of stimulating sexual energy, leading it through *chakras* (vital centers in the body), and storing it up in the abdomen.

A book was written some years ago about *kundalini*, the vital energy that some Indian sources say lies at the root of the spinal column. The picturesque language used to describe this energy evokes the image of a serpent, released and un-coiling like a flash of lightning to the top of the head. The author, Gopi Krishna, tells in great detail how one day he was concentrating on a spot in his body, as he had done for a long time, and suddenly had an overwhelming experience that completely disoriented him. He became a victim of a process that he had triggered off, not knowing where it would lead. He had no one to help him. In a sense his unguided efforts destroyed his normal life. He could not work, he was weak, he had bouts of vivid psychic experiences. This lasted for years. He wrote that his experiments with meditation had released such a powerful flow of energy that profound changes of function and structure took place in the nervous system itself. He went on to investigate and found other cases similar to his own—including people whom he met in mental hospitals who had had such experiences from dabbling in a similar way. "Dabbling" may seem too light a word to describe the devotion that the writer gave to his early efforts, but in the sense that these efforts were unguided and unin-formed, it is accurate. A famous Chinese writer and teacher of T'ai Chi, Yearning K. Chen, said:

> It will be easy to bring forth a corrupt practice in which mind intent causes the ch'i to rise upwards, causing congestion in the brain. Eventually you will suffer from a disorder in the nervous system. The spirit will be divided internally, causing suffering from the heart and stomach ailments. If the spirit should fall then one will suffer from bleeding piles, bowels or a ruptured hernia.

These two writers, from different cultures and backgrounds, both with practical experience of what they write, warn about levels of danger on the psychological and physiological planes.

We must conclude that although *ch'i* cultivation formed part of the Taoist Way, the practical aspect of the subject can be learned only from someone who has personally followed it. This must take many years. Books and courses, apart from their theoretical interest, are a danger-ous blind alley. Instead, one should try to be as natural as possible. The idea of being natural occurs in different guises in Taoist teaching. It can act as a safety valve in the case of undue preoccupation with the sub-ject of *ch'i*. "Natural" means "more relaxed." Relaxation is important in T'ai Chi and leads to a better appreciation of having a smooth, coor-dinated, flowing movement. With the muscles more relaxed, try to sub-mit to the Form (that is, to do it as exactly as you can, without introducing variations of you own), and then *ch'i* will flow more nat-urally and the breathing more evenly. If you have had a rough conver-sation with someone earlier, you will see it in a different perspective, and your common sense and fellow feeling will be restored. This is the kind of experience that we should aim for in T'ai Chi and Push Hands, not for producing a kind of euphoria through ignorant self-stimulation. Clear thinking can also help. Thinking clearly shows us that there is a big distinction between theory and practice. Chinese medical studies along traditional lines show that *ch'i* can be affected by the right medical knowledge. Practical application of this knowledge has led to cures and the alleviation of suffering. But side by side with this verified knowledge is a whole body of traditional teaching in the form of writings and diagrams, which remains theoretical or even mythical, like the phoenix. The Chinese medical authorities are themselves open to but guarded about such works and for some time have employed statistical analysis of both Western and Chinese traditional methods. They are trying to combine the scientific approach cultivated in the West with what has been handed down for centuries in their own culture. Such a praiseworthy and intellectually honest approach contrasts strongly with the blind passing on of dangerous and half-baked "knowledge" merely read and repeated by some writers and teachers.

Another theoretically interesting idea in approaching the cultivation of *ch'i* is connected with the idea of preparation and the amount of time involved. To continue the medical analogy, our common sense tells us that a medical student is not told to go and remove someone's appendix on the first day of hospital training. The student of medicine needs more preparation, and so does the student of *ch'i* cultivation. In the spiritual paths, or Ways, such as Yoga or mystical Christianity, part of the preparation consists of purification. This idea is something that has disappeared from most popular works on these subjects. The purification can consist, on the one hand, of exercises, internal cleansing of the body, fasting, special diet, herbs, and the like, and, on the other hand, of various moral restrictions combined in some cases with sexual abstinence. Or there can be various combinations of these practices, depending on the teaching. In some monastic orders there is a rule of silence, introducing a discipline into the novice's life from the beginning, curbing the dissipation of energy through chattering. But in all these cases there is some supervision either from the teacher or from the teacher's assistants. People are not expected to understand these practices on their own, from a book or from a crash course. Such ideas read in books are, or should remain, a theory. Not only *ch'i* cultivation but also the necessary preparation for it should be approached with extreme caution. I repeat this idea only because it is so important.

During such a long and arduous process, a teacher of the right caliber can discover what weaknesses the student has in the functioning of the body, mental patterns, and emotional life. If possible, a means will be found to strengthen them; otherwise the student may be asked to leave the school or monastery. This is a safeguard for both teacher and pupil. It would be unthinkable for a good teacher to keep a student on simply for personal reasons, such as the income or payment in labor. This is easily illustrated by taking a Karate school as an example. If the teacher of a Karate school discovered that a would-be student had a weak heart or was subject to violent fits of temper, the teacher could take suitable steps to reduce or eliminate the risk such a pupil would pose to him- or herself and others. If the pupil had a weak heart or a violent temper and did not disclose it, the results could be fatal.

How to recognize a teacher? I cannot deal comprehensively with this here, but some pointers can be given. First of all there should be something indefinable about the teacher that attracts you. I don't mean that the teacher should be an interesting personality or a fascinating talker, but that there should be something about him or her that you feel you can trust. It goes almost without saying that the teacher should evidently understand more about the subject than you do. You have to be able to trust someone who is going to tell you to do things you do not understand. At the same time this trust can only go so far. After a time, what evidence is there that the teacher's instructions are producing the result claimed? This is a question you must ask yourself. If the results are not forthcoming, there is something wrong and you need to understand it. A teacher should be interested in you as a person and should know about your job, your hobbies, your family, your thoughts and feelings, so as to have as clear a picture of you as possible. It follows from this that such a man or woman cannot have hundreds of pupils listed on a computer and teach them as a uniform mass. This robs the students of the individual attention that each one needs. In times past, close pupils of a master were few in number. When the Buddha or Jesus Christ spoke to the multitudes, he was not teaching them the intimate processes of his work but giving a broad message to lift them up and awaken them. A teacher who speaks to an individual student is, as it were, reading the student's personal "file" and bases his or her words—however lengthy, however brief—on this.

We have to accept that it may take some time to find a teacher who meets these fairly stringent requirements. A student who follows this course of action can anticipate as a result the gradual development of more and more discrimination, both about teachers and teachings. The student may begin to be able to detect the more dubious teachers very quickly and less dubious (but dubious nonetheless) after a short time. This discernment will clarify, at the same time, what the student is looking for. With this point we have arrived at something positive: we do not begin our study by *doing* something; we begin by becoming clearer about what it is we want to do.

4   *Some Personal Experiences*

It was some years after I approached the study of the Solo Form of T'ai chi that I really began to go into Push Hands. My first teacher had shown me some of it, but I was also studying Karate at that time, had done Judo previously, and did not then appreciate the inherent possibilities of Push Hands. To my uninformed eye the pushing looked weak and ineffectual compared with the devastating power of Karate kicks and punches. Also, in those early days most students of T'ai Chi emphasized the *ch'i* power without really comprehending its physical manifestation through the body. We all expected that somehow our partners would fall over once we had accumulated enough *ch'i*. So I did not see the enormous dynamic potential of the art.

In performing the movement called As If Closing a Door followed by the final Crossing Hands, it is possible to sweep an attacker's kicking leg—and then his or her entire body—clean off the floor and into the air. It is unlikely that when learning the Solo Form you would see this technique hidden, as it were, in the movement. I saw almost no potential Push Hands movements in the Form and have found that my own pupils have the same experience. It is always a revelation to them, even the seasoned martial artists, when they see it for the first time.

After I had been doing pushing for a while I realized that I and my fellow students were all extraordinarily tense. As T'ai Chi is essentially a relaxed system, I reasoned that there was something wrong. Theoretically, at least, the movements should be free and open. Later I spoke to an American who had been studying Push Hands in Taiwan and Peking. I shall tone down his language a bit, but what he said was something like this: "Only masters and idiots can do Push Hands and remain relaxed. The masters can, and the idiots imagine they can." What he meant was that the beginners were behaving as though they were masters and that as a result their superficial appearance of being relaxed masked their tension. A T'ai Chi master is so relaxed as to be able to sense exactly what the other person is doing and compensate for it softly. A beginner, in an endeavor to tell what the other is doing, can only attempt it through tension. The beginner's muscles and nervous system are not yet attuned.

So in a subsequent class I tried pushing with more force. My partner went off balance right away. He was a student instructor, and it looked bad for him to lose his posture in an open class. He glared at me and said, "You are using force." Whatever interpretation one might put on my misdemeanor, the fact was that he, a potential instructor, could not cope with even a little more force than usual. It was the same for almost the entire class, no matter what the individual student's size and weight. I also tried experimenting with a number of the techniques of the Solo Form during the Push Hands sessions, and I found them effective. What eluded me for a long time was the necessary compromise between yielding too much and giving your partner sufficient resistance to push against. If you try to melt away completely, your partner cannot push and therefore cannot study. It becomes a kind of nonevent, for every time he pushes, you are not there. Moreover, if you melt away, you no longer sense where your partner is going and you have nothing to work on, whereas if you give your partner too much to push on, too much solidity, you will be sent flying.

At that time it mattered to me a great deal that I should not be uprooted. I felt that I ought to be able to handle any push I received. It was part of my image of myself—the undefeated. One night I lost my concentration and was sent backwards and upwards against the wall. I half lost my temper and swooped back at my partner, and a small struggle broke out between us, Push Hands completely forgotten. This was quickly interrupted by the instructor. Since that time my outlook has changed a lot. I know that if someone pushes me and I lose balance, it is all part of the day's work. I must profit by my mistake, invest in loss.

On another occasion I was talking to a Chinese instructor of Kung Fu, and we began to talk about Push Hands. He spoke with mild contempt about its effectiveness. He wanted to try me out and suddenly gave me a kick to the right hip—not hard but on the mark. I had not been prepared, since he did it suddenly right in the middle of our conversation. I asked him to try me out again. He launched another attack, this time with his hands. I did a movement something like Fair Lady Works with Shuttles and sent him backwards. I had moved very quickly. He did not know what had happened and said, "What was that?" I said that I thought it was a Push Hands movement.

Several incidents crystallized for me the principle of adaptability. Once I went to London's Chinatown to visit a Shaolin Kung Fu teacher and once again the conversation moved round to Push Hands. I asked him if there was anything like it in Shaolin. He pushed me a number of times. His stance was like a rock. My yielding was no use in this case. It dawned on me that I would never move him if I used the same tactics that I used on T'ai Chi students. I tried again, using more lifting power in my push, and perched him on the counter of his shop. We parted on good terms, and as I walked away to my car I wondered about the experience. I showed me that to expand Push Hands I had to try to be able to adapt to all circumstances. I might meet someone as nimble as a monkey or as solid as a house.

One day I was away from my own T'ai Chi class, and one of my students, Sean Dervan, was in charge. A T'ai Chi teacher visited, from a school teaching a different style. Afterwards I was told that the visitor was really going all out to push Sean over but did not succeed. When Sean went on the "offensive" and used as many techniques as he could find, the visitor could not cope and was repeatedly pushed away. Apparently he could only handle the type of movements that he was familiar with. This underlined for me my own thoughts about adaptability. We were at that time going into many possibilities in the class, and I began to realize that the principle of Yin and Yang is an experimental one for us human beings on the so-called conscious level. Techniques as such should be at the service of the principle; otherwise they become obstacles.

In the T'ai Chi world there are many forms of Push Hands. Some of the are downright violent. Although I know some of these, it would be inconceivable to use them in a class. But within the confines of what can be called safe techniques there are many variations, and the principle of Yin and Yang should enable one to experience these techniques and, in so doing, to find more. Timing can often be wrong, so you may be caught out by something new; but by sticking to the principle, you know you are going in the right direction.

Another example of this idea of adaptability came from a student teacher who visited our class regularly, specifically to train at Push Hands. His approach was utterly defensive. He would stand almost in a crouch, his body and arms rounded so that it was difficult to move him and no flow ever developed. Eventually I decided that I had let this state of affairs continue for long enough. I decided to go straight through him. By this I mean that instead of following his semirigid arms and being led far outside the circle of his normal defense, I would push straight through his arms into his body. This I did. He had no set answer to it, apart from flailing at my arms with his, and so he lost balance. I kept on and on at him until we were both tired. Then we talked about it. I hoped that by being subjected to repeated attacks of this kind he would soften his approach and become more intelligent about what he was doing.

About forty years ago the world of Judo competition was not the mauling circus it is today. Judo students stood up relatively straight, with a good posture, and tried their techniques. Bending over near double, fighting with the jacket swinging about like a forgotten towel, and so on were really frowned upon. There was more emphasis on Judo and less on winning. Recently, in 1988, Push Hands competitions have begun to make their appearance in the West. The signs are that they will go the same way as Judo. They say that anything human beings can think of to do—whatever it is—they will, unfortunately, do it. So I see that competitive Push Hands is here to stay. Those of us who wish to see a different approach to the art preserved must simply preserve it ourselves and not waste our energy criticizing others.

Very often, when teaching T'ai Chi, I have been struck by the very short span of everyone's attention, including my own. This has improved over the years, but I ought to try to explain. Someone pushes you and you yield; the other follows up with a continuous advance and you yield again. Your partner is very active and enters with yet a third push. There has been no letup and you have been unable to counter. At the third push you are unable to yield and you "freeze." His push sends you off balance. The intriguing question is, Why can't you continue to follow and yield? There is some kind of buildup from the first push. It is like having a bad day. First you wake up late in the morning, then your car won't start, and when it does there is a colossal traffic jam. Your bad mood grows worse because you are unable to defuse the situation. In a matter of seconds the same thing happens in Push Hands. One of the reasons for this is the deep fear we have of losing our balance. This interrupts our attention. Moshe Feldenkrais, the famous teacher of posture and movement, studied Judo at one time and based some of his ideas on the theory that most adults, unlike little children, are afraid of falling, and therefore fall. He advocated the study of Judo to help overcome this fear. In Push Hands it is rare actually to fall to the floor, and we all know this, yet the fear of losing one's balance steals the attention away and brings about what one is trying to avoid.

They say that a drunk does not fall with as much injury to him- or herself as a sober person. I do not advocate drinking alcohol before T'ai Chi training, but there is something to be learned from this. The drunk does not care about falling. It is all one: standing, falling, sitting, lying—what's the difference? The drunk is beyond worrying about such trifles. A drunk has parted company with self-image. Psychologically, then, there is nothing left to protect. A student of T'ai Chi who was like this would not care about not being a "master." So our fear of falling together with our need to protect our image of ourselves pose a considerable challenge to the discipline we are trying to understand.

While on the subject of difficulties, let us look at the idea of being rooted. One's usual psychological center of gravity is too high, around the chest and the head. In practical terms, we are usually not aware of the lower body and the legs. The famous comic strip hero Superman is a narrow-waisted, broad-shouldered figure. Everything in him points upwards, like a triangle with its apex on the ground. We know he is not rooted, since he can fly. Rootedness is not conducive to flying. T'ai Chi theory bids us cultivate rootedness by sending our awareness down the body and staying low in our bodies. But when beginners hear of this intention, they often interpret it by stiffening themselves and tilting the pelvis forward, thus losing balance backwards. I have tried to wean my students from this error by pointing out that the vertebrae that make up the pelvic area are part of the back and that it is a mistake to try to make an artificial joint between the lumbar and sacral vertebrae. Becoming rooted is all part of the effort to let go of the tensions in the body so that it can be allowed to respond to the pull of gravity quite naturally and go downwards towards the earth.

Reading or hearing about the *theory* of T'ai Chi and rootedness can have an adverse effect if it causes the mind to become too involved and the *ch'i* to rise upwards towards the brain. Then the body is not free to function by responding to the constant, stabilizing force of gravity. I have often thought in this connection of Bob Hope in the film *The Paleface*. Hope is going out to meet a famous gunfighter, and he is useless at gunfighting. So everyone gives him advice like, "He leans to the left, so shoot to the right," "The wind will be in the east, so shoot to the west," "The ground slopes down so shoot up," and so on. Hope is seen approaching the fight contorting his body and muttering all this advice, totally mixed up. Ideally, then, I ought to throw away all books and give out one idea per year. But this good piece of Taoist advice would not be met with open arms by most students.

T'ai Chi is international, and I have had several visits from students from the United States. One of these was an attractive woman from the East Coast who had been studying with a well-known teacher: "My teacher does this, my teacher does that; in the States we do it this way and that way." Once more we were faced with a locked mind. Should we be old-fashioned and behave like ladies and gentlemen and not push her? We pushed her just enough to make her think again. She never came back. A pupil of a pupil of Cheng Man-ch'ing was the same in a way. Whatever technique members of our class tried, he would always do Rollback. Sometimes this worked, but after a few minutes I simply used moves on him that Rollback would not answer. His was not a case of mental prejudice. Somehow his reflexes had become so ingrained that he could not learn anything else. I did not feel any criticism towards him, just amazement. He literally could not learn anything new. He smiled sheepishly, apologized, and went on using Rollback. This is not an unchanging pattern. Some students learn very quickly. I had one student who could do Push Hands well after three weeks. He gave my best students a hard time within six seeks. With me though, possibly because I was the teacher, he had a block, and was unable to act as freely as with the others.

Two small rules of mine are worth mentioning. If I go to see a T'ai Chi teacher in his or her own training hall, I always allow the teacher to push me. I consider that even the best of teachers would not wish to lose face in his own school. For good or ill I let the status quo stand. A second rule is that if a man comes to learn and brings his girlfriend with him to watch the first time, I never push him with any degree of effort. His girlfriend is there, and he feels under extra pressure to show up well. If the girl joins the class as well, then it is business as usual. A touch of Confucian decorum in a Taoist discipline.

As I said in *The T'ai Chi Workbook*, my first style was the Yang style. When I met a Wu-style teacher, she told me I was wrong, so for a time I suspended Yang style to learn Wu. Gradually I found more and more variations. It was not long before I became quite open to any difference in interpretation of a movement provided it made sense. Then, as my classes' experiments in T'ai Chi Push Hands deepened and several students visited Singapore and Malaysia, bringing back further methods with them, we began to see that movements from other styles of internal martial arts had their place. That is to say they had their place in T'ai Chi. One of these movements is illustrated in photos 114–121. It came about in the following way. We were trying pushing off balance against the outside of the shoulder, a little towards the back. We found various methods of yielding to this, from the simplest slight movement to complete body shifts. Then we experimented with turning in a circle away from the push and lifting the hands to push as the circle was completed. It looked remarkably like Pakua, the Eight Trigrams school of internal martial arts. It may not be exactly what Pakua students do, but it is similar. In our small experimental world this small discovery was great. We suddenly saw meaning in the photographs of this other art that we had never studied. A man with his right hand reaching almost round to the left back at waist level and his left hand raised to shoulder level—we had all seen such photographs, but I for one had never thought about it because Pakua was outside my field of study. And then there we were, doing it simply through experiment. If I stuck only to what I had been told, I would never have found this out. It would still be just Rollback, Press, and Push and nothing else.

This brief description of some experiences and thoughts will, I hope, be some small inspiration to you in your own Push Hands, both in forms presented in this book and in your own experiments.

5   Stories and Sayings

One of my favorite stories tells how a famous master used to feed the birds. He would let them settle, one at a time, on the palm of his hand. When a bird was about to fly away, it needed some firmness for its feet to press against in order to launch itself. The master was so sensitive and his yielding so refined that he could detect even the tiny muscular effort of the bird's legs, and each time it began to push against his palm he yielded just enough to prevent it from flying away.

In bygone days the students of a famous master found that they were unable to follow his movements. He almost never spoke to them but simply showed them with his body a few times and waited for them to learn. They discussed the problem with one another for several years, and on one of these occasions the seven-year-old brother of one of the students was there listening to what was said. Unknown to the students, the master himself was standing behind a screen, taking in what they were saying. At one point there was silence, and the seven-year-old took the opportunity to speak: "If you can't copy what he does, why don't you ask him to explain?" The elder brother whirled on the youngster to reprimand him, but at that moment the voice of the master was heard to say, "What an excellent idea. Why didn't you think of that?"

Someone asked Wang Tsung-yueh how a student could tell which master was teaching the Yang style correctly and which was wrong. He replied, "Centered, straight, comfortable, relaxed."

Chen Wei-ming said, "Your internal strength will grow the more you relax, the more you become loose. Internal strength should animate your body in T'ai Chi, not the muscular strength you use to do manual work. Study this."

26

There were many discussions about the Tao, about Ch'an (Zen) and the origins of Ch'an. Chinese students could not accept that it came directly from India. They said that it was too Chinese and not Indian in its approach. They said that Ch'an was the result of the interaction of Indian Buddhism and Taoism. If this is so, then T'ai Chi, a Taoist art, has definite affinities with Zen from a historical as well as a psychological view.

A certain teacher, living today, taught his students, "The man who does not seek to struggle [fight] with others will find that others are not able to struggle with him. Think of still water. You push it, and, yielding, it finds its original place. Air should be thought about too. It yields so softly you do not even notice the change." A Western visitor more forward than the Chinese students replied, "But sir, we are not water or air. How can this apply to us?" The master smiled: "You are almost all water and air, but your ego is iron." T'ai Chi is about returning. The Japanese symbol of the pliant willow that gives way to the weight of snow, lets it fall, and returns to its original place is like that. The circle, found in all traditions, is a universal symbol of return. In Push Hands we return many times through many points in circles or curves. Returning is almost like not moving, like stillness.

Amazing claims are made about the abilities of T'ai Chi masters. Robert Smith, in his book *Chinese Boxing Masters and Methods*, tells how a young woman asked the renowned Cheng Man-ch'ing how it was that her own teacher could drive her back from him without even touching her and even make her bounce up and down. Cheng laughed at all this. "I knew Li," he said. "His T'ai Chi was not too good. He could do the thing you mention but only because you are a student. The trick will not work against an equal or a superior."

Yang Lu-ch'an developed the Yang style of T'ai Chi to a high level. He met many challenges and was undefeated after eighteen contests with different martial arts masters. He was given the title of Yang the Unbeatable or Unsurpassable. Like most Chinese, he wanted to pass something of himself on to his two sons, Yang Pan-hou and Yang Chien-hou. He adopted an approach that we would not associate in any way with such a gentle art. His severity was as famous as his skill. He knocked his sons down, made them bleed, split their lips, and doled out injuries with great generosity. The youths were not even allowed outside the precincts of the family home. Yang Pan-hou once scaled the wall to escape the regime but was found and brought back. Yang Chien-hou tried to hang himself and was found just in time. After this near catastrophe Yang Lu-ch'an relented and allowed that each of his sons should be approached differently, learning the art at his own speed, according to his talents; and so the master brought the spirit of the art into his relationship with his sons.

Though the father drove his sons hard, neither of them was his senior student. When Yang Lu-ch'an died his senior student, Chen Hsiu-feng, had no sooner returned from the funeral than he stepped forward and proclaimed himself the successor. The two sons had not acquitted themselves well enough in the art, so it fell to him to preserve and continue the high standard that the master had maintained. The brothers did not welcome this move but knew they were no match for Chen and bided their time. What they had refused during their father's life they now wished for after his death. They remembered the saying that ten years is not too long to wait. They regretted that they had not trained harder while their father was alive to teach them, and so set to improving their skill at once. After three years they sought out Chen and challenged him. Chen appeared to be downcast when he heard the brothers speak, but suddenly, using the energy that his training had given him, he reached out and with one hand easily lifted a huge armchair into the air and put it down by the brothers. "Use this as the head student's chair," he said, and walked away. He had used only his palm to lift the chair, and seeing this the two sons were amazed. But as Chen had so graciously yielded up his place to them, they bore him no ill will.

The history of T'ai Chi during the early part of the nineteenth century is somewhat hazy. But there is a story that a large school where T'ai Chi and meditation were taught existed on the outskirts of Shanghai. The teacher in charge was a certain Chen Po-ho, famous for his knowledge of Ch'an. His leading student had received an extensive Western education and was a Christian. This Christian was also something of an intellectual and bookworm. He always asked many questions, and his studies in the internal arts had led to an accumulation of books, notes, scrolls, and paintings of past masters. At the same time he realized that his T'ai Chi was not at a level that would qualify him really to fill the master's place when the time came. In particular his Push Hands was not at a high level. Chen had told him how to study and what he needed, but to no avail. He was still unable to uproot another person cleanly, always exerting too much muscular force. He decided to try once more during one particular evening training session. After training in the Form, the moment for Push Hands came. Chen's small daughter was a member of the class, and the Christian student was told to practice with her. In amazement he took up a position opposite her, her head some two feet below his own. When he put his hands on her arm, it seemed to him that there was nothing there. Her arms floated beneath his like passing clouds. Suddenly he realized that he was moving backwards. A flash of panic shot through him and in that moment he was uprooted, hurled back against the wall. The entire class turned and looked at him. He stood up. For some reason his mind was completely clear of any confusion or shame at being thrown by such a diminutive partner. From that day on he understood the comment he had so often heard and even more often read: "Relax, just relax."

It is difficult to follow the maxim that the mind should control the body. The body seems to have a mind of its own. The same maxim is found in Oriental swordsmanship. If you intend to meet the sword as it moves to strike you, your mind will adhere to the sword and you will be cut. These words, said to have been uttered by the Zen master Taku-an, imply that when the mind freezes at the sight of the sword, the body freezes too. For the mind to control the body rightly, the mind itself must first become free, and then it can direct the body. Therefore, in Push Hands, when you receive a push, do not freeze at the impression of the force because this will make the body freeze and you will be uprooted. Keep your mind moving and your body will be free to move also. If you observe your Push Hands you will see this tensing or freezing taking place in you time and again. The reaction of saving one's balance by tension is in fact one of losing one's balance. When someone asked Cheng Man-ch'ing why none of his pupils could equal him, he said that they had no faith. They had no faith in the principle of yielding. Another teacher said, "When two men push hands they must recognize the Yin in them, and when two women push hands they must recognize the Yang in them.

It is reported that Cheng modified the T'ai Chi Form to save time. He cut out many repetitions of movements and made it shorter. His very famous Form, known simply as the Short Form, does not use all known movements of T'ai Chi. For instance it leaves out Parting Wild

Horse's Mane. With the spread of the teaching of this Form, I have observed, has also spread an ultrasoft way of doing Push Hands. The Form is taught very softly and somehow students have received the notion that pushing can be learned in this same soft way. But no tension does not mean no force. Cultivating the Yin does not mean neglecting the Yang. In addition to Yin and Yang, a third element is needed: change. Yin and Yang are two extremes but at times they are very close, especially at the moment of change. Yielding becomes pushing and pushing becomes yielding. In a Push Hands session the times between the changes vary. In the Form the time is even and continuous. You do not have to take a partner into account. With a partner you never know when a change will come. It is like life itself, in a microcosm. You never know when the phone will ring, when you will slip on a banana skin or fall in love. If you try to make yourself secure at all costs in life then you cling either to the Yin or the Yang. But life, like Push Hands, is a matter of change.

Chen Po-ho said, "Yin and Yang must be seen in both large and small. Anyone can see it in the entire body's movement, but what about something smaller? In the elbow, for instance, we can see it. When someone pushes my elbow down, then my hand comes up to neutralize. It must always happen. When one thing goes down another comes up. Study this." The venerable teacher T. T. Liang wrote, "Today everyone is too aggressive. No one wishes to yield. Everybody wishes to take advantage of others. This is common in all societies and all countries. . . . If everyone learned to relax, yield and lose, this predicted third world war would be avoided."

Master Liang inspired many students with his teaching. In particular he touched Stuart Alve Olson and Jonathan Russell. They felt the practical nature of his study of T'ai Chi when they were more than once put in difficult life situations by him. He did it to show them something about themselves. This is rare today. It depends on the teacher's being what Carlos Castaneda called "immaculate." The teacher puts the teaching before him- or herself. The students, though necessary to the teacher in a sense, are not used for profit, or self-aggrandizement or ego and this develops a sense of trust. The students will accept from the teacher, for the sake of their understanding, what they would not accept from another. Such a one has become the teaching itself.

There are other teachers who, in my opinion, are almost insane. Their cultivation of *ch'i* has become mixed up with all kinds of ordinary impulses and ambitions like greed, ego-tripping, the desire to be seen as a master teacher, and self-delusion. This is a debasement of T'ai Chi and the wisdom that surrounds it. It leads people astray, giving them the wrong impression, and will eventually poison them instead of lifting them up. It is up to each student to try to perceive the character of the teacher as soon as possible.

There is no doubt that practitioners of internal arts can display phenomena that are unusual. Some enthusiasts regard them as verging on the miraculous. Let us leave aside ancient anecdotes that cannot be verified and stick to modern eyewitness accounts, bearing in mind that even these are frequently mistaken, as any court or police officer will verify. One of these phenomena is the capacity to produce heat from the palm of the hand. You may yourself, if you train correctly and regularly, experience an overall surface body heat due to improved circulation. People who can produce this palmar heat have learned to concentrate it in specific parts of the body. I don't regard this as miraculous or mysterious but simply as a matter of training. Another example is the capacity to withstand powerful blows to the abdomen. Some T'ai Chi teachers can lie on the floor and let a student jump on to their abdomen from a height of six feet. But in the film *Kings of the Square Ring*, kick boxers and wrestlers in Japan are shown using training techniques just as rigorous as this feat as a regular part of their schedule, not as a one-time display. It is a matter of conditioning. Western performers like the strong man Sandow, the escapologist Houdini, and others have done the same thing. The fact is that by concentrating a great deal of energy at a particular place the body can withstand much more than usual. An old music hall act was for a strong man to tear a London telephone directory in half. This looks amazing if you do not know how to do it. But with a little experimenting it is easy. You either break the spine of the directory and tear from the spine or you make sure that the open edge of the directory is skewed to an angle so that you are not tearing hundreds of pages simultaneously but through one page at a time so to speak. I have done it myself and I am no Hercules.

A further example is that of influencing a student without even touching him. In my opinion—and I am open to correction—this comes from the special teacher-pupil relationship that develops over a period, as Cheng Man-ch'ing observed. A pupil is usually wide open to the suggestions of the teacher. The student is used to being put right, to following instructions. If a bit credulous, the student believes everything the teacher says without questioning. The student is used to being pushed off balance by the teacher and in due course comes to accept that he or she can never "beat" the teacher at anything. Body and brain become conditioned to react as the passive member of the relationship. I have had this experience with my own pupils and have tried to correct it. It can happen that hardly touched, a student moves back out of habit. The word *hypnotism* springs to mind, or *brainwashing*. I am sure that one of the weight lifters from the room adjacent to our class, pushed in the same way, would hardly budge. The weight lifter would not be in tune in the same way.

A final word, about being "immovable." Some teachers demonstrate, in T'ai Chi or in Aikido, how they cannot be moved from a fixed stance or that their extended arm cannot be bent at the elbow. This capacity is attributed to the use of *ch'i* (Japanese, *ki*) and not to mechanics, where it rightfully belongs. The scenario for remaining immovable is that the teacher stands in a particular stance and, say, six students line up one behind the other and push together against the teacher. This looks impressive, but in fact the total push exerted is not the sum of the individual pushes of each person. The pushing power is dissipated as it passes through each person so that the front person's hands are not giving the teacher nearly as much force as it might seem. If a rope were tied around the teacher and a trained tug-of-war team still could not move him or her, it would be something else altogether. I have not seen that yet. The unbendable arm has been shown by a well known T'ai Chi teacher in London. The teacher extends his arm sideways and rests the wrist on the shoulder of the student. Two pupils then try to press down on the elbow and bend it. They use a lot of force. The success of remaining unbendable depends in fact on the angle of the bones of the elbow joint. If the palm of the teacher is kept in a vertical plane, the pupils would have to dislocate the elbow to succeed. Not many people can exert that amount of strength from shoulder height, pressing down. So the bending of the arm is virtually impossible.

The last point to make about these feats is that none of them has any useful or practical value. What has value in T'ai Chi Push Hands is the study of Yin and Yang.

6   *Empty Mind*

The expression *empty mind* has been used in Western books on Zen, Taoism, and martial arts many times. But a thought-free, attentive state is not easy to attain. An empty mind is one of the aims of the internal martial arts, including T'ai Chi, and the relaxation that is also sought in T'ai Chi helps to foster it. A student of the internal arts has before him the challenge of defeating himself, his ego, rather than defeating his partner.

The hard-style martial arts, the so-called external arts such as Karate and Thai boxing, have their own challenges to the participants. To get up in front of another man or woman, knowing that you may be hurt or even knocked unconscious requires some courage—some may say, foolhardiness. But whatever the motive, whatever the judgment, the challenge is obvious. Within that challenge there are psychological demands such as keeping one's temper, observing the rules, and pacing one's energy. Furthermore, any failure on the part of the contestants to fulfill these demands is immediately obvious to the spectators.

But such fighters have been trained in their art and these demands are part of their training. However, the physical demand on their energy supply is so great that they would probably regard the state of empty mind as an impossible luxury. In T'ai Chi the position is reversed. The physical demands are comparatively small. There are no rules as such, just an accepted ban on blows, and without a lot of personal experience the spectator of a Push Hands session cannot really appreciate what is taking place. Here we have an ideal opportunity to train for an empty mind. What are the difficulties?

One school of T'ai Chi which I have met uses a particular concept—roundness—as its basic approach to Push Hands. Postures are rounded, arms are rounded, the whole attitude of the pupils is to become curved. Thus the least resistance is given to each push or pull. But if we are looking for an empty mind this emphasis on roundness can and does become a difficulty. It becomes a difficulty because roundness, instead of being seen as an aspect of the principle of yielding becomes instead a fixed idea, which takes form as a fixed body. The idea replaces the principle. This is not a hairsplitting notion but a fact. In the school I am referring to, fixed roundness becomes a straight line of resistance, internally. Here the mind is not empty, it is holding fast to something and is full of it. The pupil is round like a rain barrel. If the barrel were empty the student could yield and be pushed and return, but it is full of water, so there is no room for adaptation. Different interpretations, in physical terms, of the principles of T'ai Chi become for all of us, at one time or another, the water in the barrel. We begin with the principle and end up with the interpretation. It is interesting for me, and perhaps for you, to examine in detail what happens. The teacher explains the idea—yielding. The mind takes hold of it, the body tries to apply it, but then suddenly the reactions of the body completely fill the stage and yielding is nowhere in sight. So how to remember the yielding? In different ages, in different traditions, people have grappled with this question. In some Buddhist and Christian traditional teachings we find the idea of repetition. By repeating the words to himself, "Thinking, thinking," every time a thought arises, the Buddhist meditator tries to maintain something within himself that is free from the usual reactions. In some Zen schools the student tries to follow his or her breathing or repeats a sound. Calling on Jesus Christ as in the Russian Orthodox prayer of the heart is a similar practice. What one finds is that no fixed means is effective forever. Sooner or later the means itself becomes habitual, and the usual reactions bypass the means and reestablish themselves.

An example of this bypass can be taken from instances where, for a change, someone who has been doing Karate takes up T'ai Chi. He or she begins T'ai Chi and Push Hands. The student may accept the yielding principle but when threatened with loss of balance resorts to the stances and movements of Karate. So a teacher who is trying to instil an empty mind in pupils will make the principle of change operational.

He will never stay too long on any single aspect. He will teach something for a while and then drop it, change the approach. This will keep everyone in a constant state of questioning, uncertainty, doubt. In Korean Zen, a tradition not well documented in Western translations, the practice of questioning is encouraged. The word *questioning* was chosen in a particular translation because the word *doubt* implied indecision or vacillation. It also impled choosing between one course of action or thought and another. What the Korean teacher was looking for was a constant sense of inquiry. If a T'ai Chi teacher and students can keep this attitude uppermost in the training, they will be able to continue to move. Clearly, this suggestion is applicable on a much wider scale than just T'ai Chi study. Any fixed idea, when it conflicts with what we can call the flow of life, is bound to lead to a loss of balance. It is related to what the early psychologists called a complex.

For Western students, at least, it is possibly a mistake to introduce the idea of an empty mind early on. When someone comes to learn T'ai Chi he is looking for the Form, for something fixed that the student can do solo, and it is too much to expect the student also to be occupied with emptiness. The early stages are spent in collecting material to be used as a basis for later work, and the student needs a basis of form for his Push Hands, a structure. Later he or she can be introduced to the empty mind and constant change.

When I was a teenager I went to Paris for a short language course. I made friends with the other English boys and girls. On the last night of the course we had a party in the grounds of the college. One particular boy and I had struck up an immediate friendship, and we both liked the same girl. The lighting in the grounds was not very good, and people began to drift back inside. I glanced at the floor and saw a purse. It was a woman's purse. I picked it up. My friend saw me and came over. To find out whose purse it was I opened it, the other boy watching me. I saw that it belonged to the girl we both liked and said so. Suddenly he shouted at me from a distance of a few feet, "Why did you open that purse?," his eyes glaring. Among English people at that time you simply did not open other people's purses or bags and peer inside. He was clearly outraged and doubly angry because it was *her* purse. For some reason I was completely untouched by this outburst. I felt absolutely no reaction. I simply registered his face, his anger, his words, without changing inside myself at all. It was not contrived; it simply took place like that. His face slipped into a blank expression and then into an apologetic grin. He felt his own negativity, confused, and this changed him. We handed back the purse.

I have never forgotten this experience. I had not encountered T'ai Chi or Zen. My only reading and study had been in the Vedanta of India and the life and work of Ramakrishna. I did not associate this experience with any spiritual quest. But it showed me that it takes two to make a quarrel. He had tried to give me a heavy "push," but there was simply nothing to push—just an empty, attentive state. When he did not find the conflict he expected, he woke up to himself a little and felt at a loss. It was only much later in life that I was able to appraise the experience and repeat it again and again.

Empty mind is a long study. No one brought up in our society has much chance of absorbing it quickly. The springs of our behavior are very tightly wound up. Even if we could release them, it would be dangerous for us. So the slow tempo of T'ai Chi gives us a hint of what our attitude should be.

7 *Push Hands Training*

In following the photographs and words in this chapter, move slowly and in a relaxed way. Initially it is preferable to understand the mechanics of what you are doing rather than try to be soft or yielding. Once you have learned the movements themselves, you will have the opportunity to bring in other aspects.

Wrists

Your partner stands in front of you in the same position as yourself, close enough for you to assume the posture shown in photo 1. Here the back of her right wrist rests against your right wrist. Push forward off your back foot. Neither person moves his or her feet from the floor. Your partner, keeping contact with the back of your wrist, shifts her weight backwards (photo 2). When you find that to go forward any fur-

1   2

ther in an upright posture would cause you to overbalance, you stop moving and let her push you back. Do this a number of times until you are familiar with the movement. When you push, do not do so out of aggression. Simply take part in the physical motion. Your ankles carry the movement. The soles of the feet remain completely in touch with the ground. Don't go up onto your toes or back on your heels. You move back and forth in a straight line.

Keep your wrists joined. Your partner pushes forward. This time take your right wrist a little away to your left as you move back, turning your waist and trunk a little to the left also. In fact your body turns as a whole, not in separate pieces. (See photos 3 and 4.) As you reach the limit, or loss-of-balance point, you turn to the right to face forward again and rest your palm on your partner's wrist. You then push forward, and your partner retreats, turning to her right and returning to the center to begin the cycle again.

Note that the retreating in a straight line introduced first was purely an introductory exercise. Once you have got the idea you always aim to yield in a curve. You can experiment with the single-handed exercise by pushing and yielding upwards, downwards, left, right, or any changing combinations of these directions. Always remember that win-

3   4

ning and losing are unimportant. The interplay of Yin and Yang is what we want to discover.

Take up the positions shown in photo 5. The man on the left—L—is raising his right arm to show the position of the man on the right—R—more clearly, with regard to the cupped hand on L's elbow. In fact L would hold his arm lower down. R places his right hand on L's wrist and his left on his elbow. This hand positioning controls punching and elbowing by L and is a useful pointer in self-defence application.

R pushes forward with both palms at the same time. Once again, use the straight line at first for simplicity's sake. L yields and at the limit of the push turns his right wrist as before, but this time he brings his left palm to R's right elbow. (See photos 6, 7.) Here we have shown L raising his arm high. It could be low or in between. In photos 8–10 we show a continuation of this exercise in which both men are moving in varied directions, purely for experiment's sake and to get the feel of the possibilities. Also, a wide range of joint movement is enjoyed, giving the body greater flexibility. If you notice while moving that you have a tendency to restrict your breathing or breathe unevenly, it means you are too attached to what you are doing. In time you can become less and less attached to the results and more interested in the process. This will free tension and your breathing will benefit. Do not train for long periods at a time. Do short spells and have short breaks. This prevents tension from building up.

This introductory part is fundamental. It should be done over and over again. It contains two pillars of Push Hands movement, Ward Off and Push. Ward Off is presenting your arm to your partner, in this case to allow him to push.

8

9

10

We now move on to two more pillars: Roll Back and Press. Take up the position as shown in photo 11. R pushes and L yields to his right and back. Instead of cupping the elbow as before, L brings his left arm across with his turn (photo 12) so that the forearm catches R around or just above the elbow joint. R is turned away a little to his left. R brings his left palm to rest snugly and more or less at right angles on his right palm, the heels of the hands meeting. He presses back down the center again. (See photo 13.) L has rolled back—his first movement—and R has begun to press. As R presses, he is in touch with L's right wrist. L brings his left palm across to rest lightly on R's wrists and turns away to his left. As he turns, he slides his right palm to R's elbow and turns his left palm through ninety degrees to end up as in photo 14. He pushes once again, and R meets this action by beginning to roll back (photo 15). He continues to move through the same sequence in reverse as L turns his push into a press and so on (photo 16).

The whole movement traces an elongated figure eight through a horizontal plane. R is taken to his left, back to the center, forward to

11   12

13

14

15

16

Figure 2

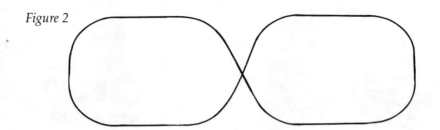

his right, back to the center, yielding to his left, back to the center, yielding to his right, back to the center. (See figure 2 for a clearer idea.)

The movements in this last sequence are a big step from the simple first ones. They do illustrate that in T'ai Chi we aim to do nothing, that is, not to add anything. If you can follow the instructions and not invent actions of your own, you will see how naturally your hands fall into place. This is particularly true in the final phase of the movements in which you will see that in turning away to your left your partner's Press will be led away under your left armpit and does not need to be dragged or pulled there. This last is a frequent fault of beginners who cannot resist "helping" the partner away to the left instead of simply allowing the partner's own momentum to do the work. It is then simple to slide the right hand to the partner's right elbow ready to begin again. Practice it very slowly and let the hands fall into place.

It should be mentioned that in Push Hands we aim never to lose contact with one another. As we go on we hope to become more and more sensitive to every movement of our partner and this is achieved by sensing, mainly through the palms of the hands, the other's constantly changing point of balance. The constant interplay of arm and hand options are like the coiling of two snakes. Push Hands can take on a more violent form, and in this case the arms become more like the powerful beating of the wings of a crane. T'ai Chi is said to have been inspired by the movements of a snake that defeated a crane in combat. Though the snake prevailed, this did not prevent some movements of the graceful bird from also being included in the Form. So if you keep in mind the idea of sinuous movement, it may help you to slide in and out of the various positions more readily.

Usually Push Hands is done for many months with the feet not moving; but as books do not contain months, we can move on to this now and leave it to your own judgment to decide when you introduce it into your training. If you stick in a foot-fixed approach for too long, you will find it hard to transfer to a more mobile approach. Experiment with both. So try all the previous sections with synchronized steps. As you take a step forward with a push, with your left foot your partner yields, stepping back with the right. Then your partner steps forward with the left, pushing in turn, and you step back with your right. Do not be confused by the new arrangement of arms and legs. Just let it flow, and the arms will take care of themselves. Then go through everything you have tried up to now with the left foot and left arm leading. Confusion may be the order of the day at first, but it will help your understanding of Push Hands if you and your partner sort it out together. Having gone through all these combinations you will have quite an array of different movements in your repertoire.

We can move on. In photo 17, R has pushed L and this time L brings his left hand right under both of R's arms and is bending his wrist upwards a little so that he can press to his left and take R's arms away in that direction. As he does so he slides his right hand back to his right side and stands ready to push R. R is ready to repeat the same action in response (photo 18). You will realize that now he is not going to push R's forward right arm, as in all the previous movements, but his rear left arm. This feels awkward at first, but you will soon get used to it.

17   18

All these lefts and rights seem hard to follow on the printed page but once you have a partner it will become clearer what is meant. Bear in mind at the beginning, too, that the movements of Push Hands should be slow and even so that you experience the changes and shifts in balance clearly and distinctly. If you rush, you will miss all this, and though you may be able to go through the motion, you will not appreciate what is taking place. Don't become imprisoned by habit. A variation on the last sequence is to bring the hand *over* the two arms, bending the wrist downwards to take the arms away.

These techniques up to now provide students with a basis on which to build further methods of Push Hands. Before we go on to them it would be useful to look at some of the details of performance. Let us assume that you can confidently carry out everything described so far and can visualize what takes place in each one.

Palms of the Hands

We all know, intellectually at least, that the human hand is capable of some of the finest and most delicate work imaginable. It can also heal, soothe, build, and destroy. For most of us it is not called upon to do very much. We usually admire the work of other men and women's hands. What we can learn from Push Hands is something about the sensitivity of the palms and fingers—particularly the palms, because it is the palms that should make the most contact with the partner. It is dangerous to try to push with the fingers, as the joints can easily be damaged. Like any part of the body, the palms are very responsive to our attention. If you put down this book and look at your own palm— become aware of it— you will appreciate that there is life there, intelligent life. Then slowly rub both hands together, trying to be as sensitive as possible to each. Surely you must admit that in general you are not noticing at all the intelligence and life in your own hands. Yet with training you might perform a delicate surgical operation, do the most exacting and detailed drawing, or any number of other tasks requiring a cultivated hand.

When you touch your partner, your beginner's mind is intent on pushing and all that it conjures up. But we do not want that. We are looking rather for the touch associated with a lover, a mother, or someone who like animals. One who loves to make crafts contacts the work through the palms and fingers. The love—which is a feeling—works in harmony with the body. So when you touch your partner with your own palms, you try to bear in mind the craftsman and his work. Your partner is in a sense your material, and you are your partner's. Then the mind needs to be watchful so that everything will work more in harmony. Untrained and alone, the body will just push. With care it will push more sensitively, and with an alert mind you will not forget so quickly. I think this is a good analogy that can be used to help Push Hands develop.

Soles of the Feet

Far away from the appreciative hand are the soles of the feet. In general they are far less noticed than the hands, but since we push from them we should pay more attention to them. You may not be generally aware of how you stand. By that I mean that you are not sure where most of your weight is when standing up straight, on what part of the soles. Some people stand rocked back on their soles, others stand falling inwards on to their arches, and still others stand on the sides of their feet or rocked forward. I have been told by people who specialize in the study of posture that it is bad to cave in towards the arches and rock back or forwards. It is better to find a point just back from the middle of the foot—which approximates to an important acupuncture point. It is impossible to be specific about this, but it deserves attention. Becoming more aware of the soles of the feet improves the balance in Push Hands and helps one to remember that pushing originates there and not in the arm muscles. It is also helpful to massage and manipulate the feet and find out through touch how they are constructed. Massaging the feet is very restful and can give renewed energy.

Elbows

In T'ai Chi the elbow is never fully extended. This avoids tension and also leaves you some "push" in reserve. An arm that is still bent has some extension left in it. An extended arm has none. The position of the elbows is something that makes a lot of difference in basic Push Hands but even more in more advanced Push Hands. As a rule we aim to keep the elbows down—not contracted down but naturally allowed to drop. When you put your hands on your partner's arms, you let your elbows down. This is a natural position for pushing a door that is stuck or a car that won't start. With elbows down you can transmit the force that comes from your legs and back more easily through your arms and into your palms. In more advanced techniques your partner will push your body or pull you by the elbow. It is much more difficult for your partner to reach your body if the elbows are down. It is also harder for the other to disturb your balance. Just experiment, and you will quickly see the sense in that.

The Knees

In T'ai Chi a lot is demanded from the knees and also from the thigh muscles. With time your thigh muscles will become strong through this training—strong but not bulky. Through constantly stretching and releasing the thighs a very high standard of muscle quality is reached. Even very elderly students of T'ai Chi have excellent flexibility in this region of the body. An oft-mentioned rule in T'ai Chi is that we aim not to let the knee come forward beyond the toes when we bend the leg. If you take up the standard Push Hands posture and begin to bend your leg more and more so that the knee extends beyond the toes, you will begin to experience a lot of strain at the knee. When you push back with your bent leg to return to a more comfortable position, you will find it more difficult than following the rule of not going beyond the toes' position. If your partner were to pull you forward from the beyond-the-toes position, you would find it nearly impossible to recover your balance, as your center of gravity would be too far extended.

In the beginning of training you will find it useful to massage your thighs and around your knee joints to prevent stiffness and increase circulation. The kneecap itself can be moved around, with the leg in a relaxed, extended position.

Shoulders

Over ten muscles are attached to the scapula, from different directions. The shoulder, therefore, is a big center of activity, tension, and relaxation. When you are pushing hands, you should try to let the shoulder blades move freely over your rib cage and not fix the muscles. When you are pushed at the wrist and elbow, allow the blades to move down as you lead your partner away.

Training in this method will give you a surprising degree of mobility that can be tested by a small experiment. Take the standard posture and let your arm be pushed as usual. Instead of retreating with the trunk and arm combined, just let the arm itself move back in a curve, letting your shoulder blade carry the movement. Then try the same action but ask your partner to push up at an angle of forty-five degrees. As he does so, keep your legs and body still and take your shoulder blade up, round and down. In more advanced techniques of Push Hands this shoulder blade action can be used very effectively to upset your partner's balance and leave him or her open to a counterpush from the side that will be difficult to cope with. To let the shoulders become more free, raise and rotate them and lower them, as an exercise. With patience and experiment you will soon find the amazing flexibility of this part of the body, which can also lead to a greater ease in breathing. This exercise is known to help elderly people with hypertension when combined with T'ai Chi Form training.

Hips, Abdomen, and Waist

Since I seem to be saying that everything is important, how can anything be important? The point is, each region of the body is important as it comes into play. Loosening and freedom in waist movement is vital in T'ai Chi Form and Push Hands. In Zen training and in Chinese writings on meditation, as well as in the T'ai Chi Classics, the abdominal region is stressed again and again. The Japanese refer to the *hara* and the Chinese to the *tan tien*, and both mean either a specific point in the abdomen or the general area. When you perform the exercises or techniques in this book you always need some waist-abdominal movement, however slight, since every movement requires the body to move as a whole. Learn about the waist by turning slowly, to avoid injuring the lower back. Some schools of T'ai Chi teach a tucking in of the sacrum. But this may be a misinterpretation of the instruction to *lower* the sacrum. What was meant to be achieved through relaxation people accomplish through tension, tucking the sacrum forward. Unless you have analyzed your own movements, you may not be aware of how much action the lower part of the trunk can produce. If you sit on a chair with your feet flat on the floor and extend both arms forward at shoulder level, you can try turning your trunk-waist to the right. If your arms move only a few degrees, your present possibility is small. If you manage, say, seventy degrees, it is fine. Then try extending your arms with scapula movement only. Depending on your size, you can move the fingertips forward some nine to fifteen inches without moving the body.

A strong and flexible abdomen can have a beneficial effect on your general confidence and outlook. I do not mean that it is a panacea. But if, for instance, you feel worried or weak in the face of the demands of daily life or a sudden shock, it can be beneficial to perform some waist movements to firm up the abdomen. It acts as a kind of pillar, if you will, on which the rest of the body stands. Without a firm and flexible abdomen, your T'ai Chi will be weak.

Back and Head

The instructions for the back and head are simple: keep them naturally straight, if possible relaxing the lower part of the back. In most styles of T'ai Chi the back is held upright and the head straight on top of it, eyes horizontal. This is the position for the standard posture and in 99 percent of the movements this posture is to be maintained. Otherwise the balance is more easily lost. Take, for instance, a situation in which you push forward with both hands or are pulled by a partner. The usual, untrained action is to lean forward. This means that the head, the heaviest part of the body by volume, goes beyond the center of gravity. The balance is therefore strongly upset in a forward direction. The rest of the body follows the head, as night follows day. If, instead, you move the whole body forward, keeping an upright posture, your position with respect to your balance is unchanged, even though you have moved forward. Try it and find out. The point about keeping the eyes forward is simple: you can see.

If you follow the pointers explained above, your Push Hands will improve along the right lines. In not, you will find it hard going.

8   *More Push Hands*

Some of the exercises or training methods in this section are the out-
come of experiments in Push Hands in my classes. They are aimed at
familiarizing students with using the movements of the Form in a
repetitive way that provides continuity. In other books including some
Push Hands training, a Form movement is often shown as one of application. These applications are fine. What I was looking for—and still
am—are methods that students can study and perform time after time
without having to stop and come back to a starting position. The first,
and, to some extent, complex one for beginners is Step Back to Drive
Monkey Away. It will be useful for beginners to follow and work this
one out. Though it could be used in a combative way, please try it in
the same fashion as the earlier methods. It has the unique feature of
being a backwards-moving exercise; but to make it possible, one person moves forwards at the same time. L raises both hands and grips
your right wrist with his right hand (photo 19). You shift your weight
to pull him forwards, turning your palm face upwards and drawing
your elbow back towards your body (photo 20). You step back and he

19   20

51

steps forwards with you. At the same time you bring your left arm forwards and down to press his elbow joint. (photos 21, 22.) You can see that you have roughly gone through the Drive Monkey Away movement.

To continue the sequence unbroken L reaches over with his left hand and grips your left wrist (photo 23). You shift your weight back (photo 24). Your partner can step in towards you, or he can step back. Whichever course he follows, you continue to reach over and press his elbow, having turned your palm upwards (photo 25).

Shoulder Stroke

The Shoulder Stroke movement from the Form is not widely understood as an application. This is because many teachers either do not teach Push Hands or, if they do, wait until students know the Form before teaching it. As a large percentage of students leave after learning the Form, the lack of understanding about application of Form move-

21   22

23

24

25

ments to Push Hands is understandable. Shoulder stroke is perhaps the most powerful move of the Form and so should be done with caution. One useful safeguard will be shown below.

From the usual Ward Off and Push position, R simply lowers his right arm and raises his left (photo 26). As he does so he steps in, between L's legs, and pushes him away with the shoulder. To safeguard himself from an unexpected impact L may raise his left palm to receive the stroke, or R, instead of using his shoulder, may push the chest with his left palm. If you are training softly, there is no danger; but sometimes the pace heats up and L could take a heavy impact. In a combat situation the shoulder transmits the full body weight; or a shrug, using the scapula, can be delivered (photo 27). To make the exercise more interesting it can be varied by L's raising his left palm and turning R away (photo 28). In response R dips and turns to his right to yield to L (photo 29). R continues to turn to face L (photo 30). R steps outside L and raises his left arm as in Ward Off Left (photo 31). He can continue to ward off and either send L backwards or throw him over his

26   27

28

29

30

31

left leg (photo 32). As an alternative, the action of Diagonal Flying Posture can be used to similar effect. (photo 33.)

Golden Rooster Stands on One Leg

We can combine this movement with Single Whip Squatting Down. It is the most strenuous movement. If you are not used to doing the Form, do not squat down very deeply or you will strain your legs and knees.

Say that your partner, R, pushes a little ahead of himself (photo 34). L steps back, grasping R by the right forearm (photo 35). L's body weight as he squats down pulls R forward in a bend (photo 36) and either he loses balance or pulls back. If effective in his pull back, R can be followed by L into a Golden Rooster type of movement, raising his right foot in a symbolic kick to the groin. L then steps down and pushes R, and R carries out the same sequence of L. (See photo 37 for final position.)

32   33

34

35

36

37

It must be admitted that this is purely a training exercise contrived to give both students the experience of squatting down and standing on one leg. It builds strength in the legs and helps with balance. Simultaneously, constant contact must be maintained between both.

Fair Lady Works with Shuttles

This picturesquely named movement from the Form hides a useful Push Hands move. It can be used high or low. If L pushes R with a rising action, R yields upwards and out to her right corner (photo 38). R continues to let her right arm carry up and to the side and synchronizes this Yin action with a push with her left palm—Yang—to L's chest (photo 39). In the interests of continuity of training we can carry on with a variation. As R pushes (photo 39), instead of letting her make contact, L lowers his right arm and does the Roll Back movement, diverting R to her right (photo 40). Still not outdone, R puts her palms into the Press position and presses towards L's chest (photo 41), only to be diverted by another Roll Back from the left arm. She tries again, by turning back to the center, only to be met by Roll Back again (photo 42). At any stage in this sequence of Press movements R can switch to a standard Push technique to give L a chance to try the same methods on her.

38   39

40

41

42

Single Whip Using Beak Formation

The posture of Single Whip is the one that marks T'ai Chi out from other styles. This movement from the Form has provoked many interpretations and they can all be seen as valid provided they conform to the principles. We look at one here.

This utilizes the beak hand formation (photo 43). Four fingers are brought into contact with the thumb and the wrist is bent but not stiff. When R pushes L in the basic Ward Off position (photo 44), L uses his beak to divert the left arm, hooking and turning his wrist outwards (photo 45). This action frees the left wrist of L, and he snakes his palm forwards to R's chest to push. Even if R tries to push L's elbow, he can still move his arm forwards, yielding the elbow in to the center line. (See photo 46.) For the sake of continuity we can have the second sequence, in which L, instead of reaching R's chest, is diverted himself by R using the beak to turn his push away. (See photo 47.) R then pushes at L's chest in turn. This sequence can be maintained by not letting the Push movement be completed. Photo 48 shows R completing his push.

At the moment of completing the beak diversion it is also possible to utilize a two-handed pushing movement. Make the formation and use of the beak a flowing movement, running straight into the diversion of the wrist and arm. Note that the large, open movements of the Form are condensed into smaller movements during training, but for the sake of ease of viewing, we have exaggerated them in our photographs.

43   44

45

46

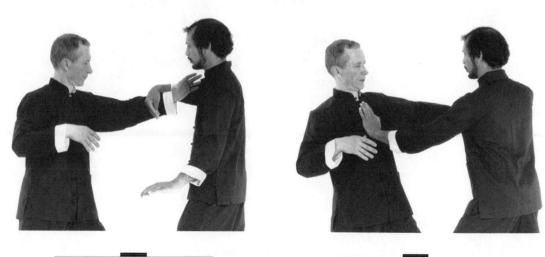

47   48

Diagonal Flying Posture

Not all the movements of the T'ai Chi Form lend themselves easily to
the cyclic ways of Push Hands. Diagonal Flying Posture is one of these,
but with some ingenuity you may be able to draw from your fund of
methods to produce examples of your own. Say that R has begun to
push you—L—and you are in some basic posture.

L steps outside R's right leg (photo 49), sweeping his left arm up high
under the right armpit. The move can be done over the arm, but since
the face might be hit, it is better for beginners to come under. If carried on, the action could take R down over L's leg. For continuity's sake
R begins to bend, bringing both arms down over L's arm (photo 50).
R then simply slides his right leg back and could send L down on to
his face. Continuing the sequence, L steps round R's right leg before
he can be put down (photo 51) and begins to step between R's legs (photo 52). His right palm presses R's elbow, and his left pushes across R's

50

51

52

chest (photos 53, 54, 55). Note that this time his left leg is between R's legs. L drives forward and back, sending R off balance. In photo 56 we show this move as if L were a taller partner. His height in this instance would make it more difficult to carry out the movement. In this case you press down on the joint just below the groin. (photo 57). He may begin to lose balance and then you can either continue to press or renew your left arm action, depending on circumstances.

53

54

55

56

57

Waving Hands in the Clouds

This pleasing movement from the Form can readily be seen as a parry to a punch to the face and the abdomen or a double push to chest and abdomen. But it can be incorporated into a Push Hands sequence in a variety of ways. In photo 58 L yields high to a basic push and at the same time pushes under R's right elbow to R's left. L lowers his right palm as in Waving Hands to push R in the abdomen (photo 59). R in turn lowers his left palm to divert L's right (photo 60). L pushes down a little on R's right elbow with his left palm (photo 61), and brings his right palm up into the basic pushing position. The sequence can then begin again with R taking the yielding role. Once you have become used to this sequence you will see other opportunities of breaking the circle and pushing in to the hip or shoulder, working in Roll Back actions to defend against it, and moving back into the Waving Hands movements. Photo 62 shows L ready to begin again.

If you have been working through these examples steadily and trying them out you will appreciate that looseness at the shoulder and elbow is important. The solid region will be the trunk, while the arms will be sensitive and mobile.

58   59

60

61

62

Like a Snake

This sequence can be done with one arm, two arms, opposite arms or corresponding arms. It employs the kind of movement we associate with a snake. You wind or coil your arm around your partner's arm and strike or push at the elbow joint. Initially join your right or left single palm to wrist. (See photo 63). As L yields to R's single pushing, he turns his left wrist outwards to divert. Keeping contact with the forearm, he slides his palm down to R's elbow (photos 64, 65). Note that he pushes on the fold of the elbow and not underneath. L continues to push the elbow back against R's body to send her off balance. To counteract this move (photo 66) R yields her left waist, turning away to her left, and brings her left palm round to push L back on the inside of his elbow, as she is beginning to do in photo 67. A variation is take your hand and arm to the outside of your partner's. Then you can try with right and left arms and with both arms combined. To concentrate your mind even more, you may try to push his left arm with your right as he tries to push your left with his right. As a break from this rather short cycle you can easily revert to the basic Push and Ward Off cycle with both

64

65

66

67

hands, to recover your composure, as well as other cycles. Remember that there are no rules as to specific movements to be used in Push Hands. There are only the principles, and any practical exploration of these principles is allowed. Do not be hemmed in by what Mr. So-and-So says. Remember that Push Hands is not an artistic exercise per se but a practical one. The artistry emerges from the practicalities.

White Crane Spreads Wings / Brush Knee

White Crane is plainly seen as a defence against a blow to the right temple and a kick or palm strike to the lower body. But for a cycle for Push Hands combined with Brush Knee try the following. Begin as in photo 68. As R pushes, L raises his right arm and pushes up and over with his left palm on R's right arm (photo 69). R yields with his right arm and continues to push back to L. As he does so L circles his left arm down and across R's pushing hands (photo 70). He takes R's arms to

his left and brings his freed right arm around and up to push R's left shoulder (photo 71). R in turn circles his right arm over and brushes L's right arm away, yielding at the right shoulder (photos 72, 73). Photo 74 is a wide open shot so that you can see the Brush Knee movement clearly. R is "brushing" his right knee and is ready to push.

Notice once again, by way of a reminder, that the elbow, wrist, and shoulder are all focal points for transmitting your push ultimately to the whole body and uprooting your partner. If you regard Push Hands movements and Form movements from this point of view you will gradually lose all sense of technique or special moves and begin to blend with the fundamental idea of Yin and Yang. You will begin to discover techniques that are not identifiable with specific movements from the Form but lie somewhere between two or three movements that they can be seen to resemble.

72

73

74

Ta Liu Push Hands

This series of moves is sometimes called the Dance and variations of it abound. We have taken one version—a short one—and broken it down into specific movements for the sake of clarity. It should be performed with flow. From the basic push position shown in photo 75 with R's hands on L's wrist and elbow, L steps back ninety degrees to his left, grasping R by the wrist and elbow (photo 76). As he steps, L pulls R forwards and steps back with feet together; R steps forwards with his left foot (photo 77). R then steps in the same direction as L, moving into Shoulder Stroke as L steps back and parries R's raised left arm with his left (photo 78). R raises his right palm to take away L's right palm, which L has raised in order to execute Push (photos 79, 80). As he diverts L's right wrist, R grips it and grips L's right elbow, stepping back at ninety degrees ready to pull. The sequence has begun again with R taking L's place. R pulls and L steps forwards (photos 81, 82, 83). As R steps back, L moves in with Shoulder Stroke, and so on. You can have lots of fun working this one out. Just remember that you have Push, Pull, Shoulder Stroke, a splitting of the arms, and the sequence begins again. The Ta Liu introduces ninety-degree changes of direction and so is important in the development of Push Hands.

75   76

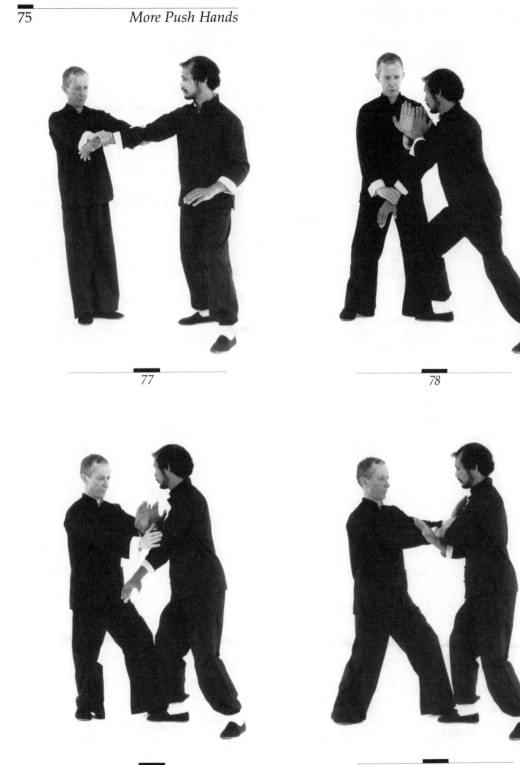

77

78

79

80

81

82

83

Separate to Go down the Middle

This movement's name is one of the most apt, as you do just what it says. It uses the simple movements of Separate the Hands and Push and demonstrates the saying in T'ai Chi that with a little force correctly applied you can deflect, or turn aside, a much stronger force. If someone is holding a long stick and pushing at you with it, to move it aside you only need a little force pushing at the end and the leverage gives you advantage. Even if he uses enormous force, it makes no difference. Similarly, when a person pushes, all his force is usually spent in one direction. We can slide or push him aside, just like the pole. In the basic push your partner could send you backwards with both palms on your chest, as R pushes L in photo 84. There is an obvious gap between her arms, and you bring your arms up, palms facing you, to separate her hands (photo 85). Do not exaggerate. You only need enough energy to take the partner's arms beyond the line of your shoulders. Circle your palms inwards so that they face your partner and push forwards

84   85

towards her elbows (or chest) (photo 86). R in turn brings her arms up the middle and pushes back on L (photo 87).

Initially, try to establish a rhythm between you so that you are able to get the flow and stick to one another more easily. Once you have got the message, or bare bones, of what to do, vary the direction of the push—upwards, downwards, to the side, and so on. You can also bring one hand up on the inside and one on the outside of her arms and push her to the right or left (photo 88). In this case R will have to take her separating arms away to her left to divert L. This sequence can easily be blended with other movements, like Brush Knee.

Smiling at Windmills

The next sequences can be done with a big smile, to help to relax, as they require almost no concentration. Smiling during a Push Hands session can be helpful. It can break up any tension that may build, whatever the reason. Take up the positions shown in photo 89. L circles his entire arm to his left and R yields. The forearms are kept in contact, with elbow, wrist, and shoulder relaxed. Continue to make a circle like two windmills. (See photo 90.) After a few cycles change direction

86   87

88

89

90

with R providing the pushing force. The shoulder blade should be allowed to move freely over the rib cage. Then change arms and do the same. Switch from left arm to right arm and right arm to left. Remember to keep the waist and knees free also, varying the action by shifting your weight backwards and forwards, left and right, and finally introduce steps so that the feeling of freedom of movement is increased. Take this exercise a little further and use both arms—right to left and left to right, respectively—making large circles. (See photo 91.)

Beginning Posture

The elbow is a focal point in Push Hands. Study elbow movement and the possibilities inherent in it. Notice that it is not only a meeting point for the upper and lower arm but also that it has a very wide range of movement. It can open and close the arm and in addition rotate the lower arm. Unlike the knee, which can only open and close the leg, the elbow gives plenty of opportunity for evasive yielding as you will see if you study it. In photo 92 L puts his palm on R's elbow. By sim-

ply raising it and moving the elbow outwards a little R can prevent this contact (photo 93). Then stand as in photo 94. You can see that this is part of the second movement of the Form, Beginning (see *The T'ai Chi Workbook*).

If L and R step in close to one another, the palms of one fit directly over the elbows of the other (photo 95). Like most things, it is obvious once you see it. L is pressing down on R's elbows with a view to pushing in towards her body and sending her off balance. To counteract this R draws her elbows in and lifts them a little, as in the Form, coming up the middle and parting L's arms. (See photo 96.) She is about to press down on L's elbows but L does the same and raises his arms to press R's elbows, (photo 97). This sequence is a natural cycle with the arms rising and falling as each person takes the initiative.

Once you have got the idea of the simple basic action of this exercise you can move into the circular action. This means that when you press down on the elbow, your partner draws the elbow back towards his body, in a curve; and when he raises them again, he moves them forward as well as up, in a continuation of the curve. See that the movement is like rowing a boat, an action appearing in some Aikido forms. Try snaking your elbows to left and right like a sidewinder.

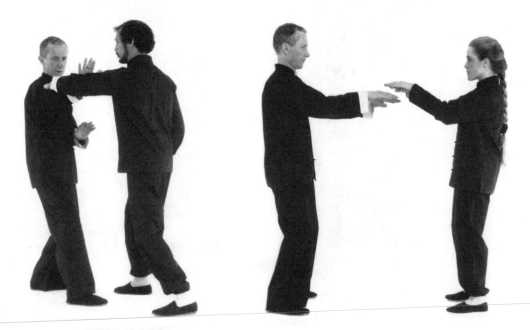

93

94

95

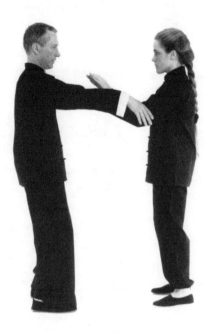

96

97

9   *Brawn . . . but Brains*

To do Push Hands well we need to be reasonably fit. Push Hands can help to make us fit, or we may be fit already. But it is a mistake to think—as some people seem to—that Push Hands is some kind of magic formula. It is also a mistake to believe that one who is as weak as a kitten can perform as well as a fit, active man or woman. We need some brawn. But more important than that is brains. This chapter is not about feelings or *ch'i* or meditation. It is about thinking—or rather alert, direct perception. Visualize your partner standing in a rectangular box as in figure 3. Imagine that the outside corners and edges of the feet follow the outline of the base of the box as in figure 4. To make this box fall over you have only to push it, but it will be easier if you push near the top. As pushing a person's head is dangerous, in Push Hands we push the next nearest point, the shoulders. The shoulders can be a target for pushing, from front, side, and back, as well as diagonally.

Unlike the box, the person has arms, and the arms and can prevent me from reaching the shoulders. When a person puts out arms as in Push Hands, with curved or bent elbows, I push the elbows, because this is in a direct line to the shoulders. A person can prevent me from reaching the elbow by using the wrist, forearm, or palm. So if this happens I push the wrist. My three targets can be seen as wrist, followed by elbow, and then shoulder. The shoulder gives me the most leverage, the elbow less, and the wrist the least. Their leverage is inversely proportional to their accessibility. The nearer the target, the less use it is to me for pushing.

It can happen that for some reason I cannot push those targets so I move lower down the box and arrive at the hips. The hips are very solid, affording very good opportunity for a push. It is harder to yield at the hips, for most of us, so although the hips are in the middle, they make up for that by giving good results when pushed. A person pushed well at the hips will take off like a rocket at the hands of a skilled partner. That is why in Taiwan where Push Hands is taken seriously

Figure 3

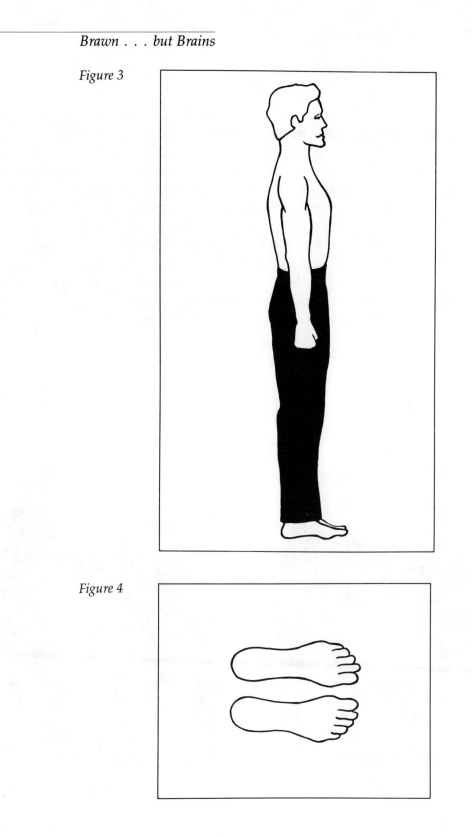

Figure 4

as a combative art, and pushing is done with gusto, there are old mattresses lining the walls so that people flying backwards will not be injured. Again, the direction on the hips can be backward, forward, sideways, and diagonal. See photo 98 in which L is indicating a diagonal, backward hip push. He is actually too far away from his partner, for the purpose of illustration. In practice he would be much closer in.

The hip push can also be given at the joint of thigh and pelvis. Still further down the box we have the knee joints. A simple downward push or slightly diagonal press with one hand at the back of the knee takes the partner down quickly and if followed by a shoulder push, will sit him on the floor. See photo 99, again with exaggerated distance. If you think, visualize and experiment with these targets for Push Hands you will learn a lot. Remember, when you push, keep up the pressure. If your partner can yield, you must gauge when to release.

98   99

The Man in the Box

Think about the person who is represented by the box. Go over the preceding moves from the partner's point of view. It is obvious, but still worth illustrating, that the box falls over because its center of gravity is moved beyond the point at which it can remain upright. (See figure 5.) Unlike the box, the person can do several things when, for

Figure 5

instance, the shoulder is pushed, as in photos 100 and 101. Your partner can turn around the vertical axis with a push, step back and take the pressure off, or sink by dropping the shoulder or by bending the knees. You partner can also use his or her arms and roll back against the inner or outer edge of your pushing arm. Please experiment for yourself on ways of yielding and defending against pushes to all targets. When I use the words *target* and *defense* here, I am not implying a fighting mode. I use them because they are intellectually clearer, more stripped-down-to-the-bone words than the Chinese words or words that are associated with T'ai Chi. Concentrate on the mechanics of what is taking place, seeing it directly.

Moving on, we can look at pulling instead of pushing. Pulling is harder than pushing in a sense because in order to pull I have to get hold and this involves just that extra bit of time and accuracy. Once again, the matter of accessibility comes up. The wrist is easier to grab and hold

102

103

104

105

because it is nearer, thinner, and lighter. The elbow is next but is harder to hold, as it is more subject to the weight of the body; but by the same token it gives more control for moving someone around. The shoulder itself is nearly impossible to hold for most people, as their hands are not big enough, but it can be pulled by pressing. Photos 102 and 103 show the wrist, elbow, and shoulder moves.

The simplest defence against pulling is to go with it. No problem? To do this requires a very high level of awareness, including a good sense of balance, readiness to yield, and no feeling of aggression or fear. No one said that simple means easy!

What is difficult for me to think about without pleasure—to be purely analytical about—is the idea of using a partner's force to upset him, the *pièce de résistance*. No principle in martial arts has been more written about and none is harder to achieve. It is the resistance of no resistance. If you look at photos 104 and 105 you see that R is pushing L on the right shoulder. R allows this push and lets it be transmitted round his back and along his left arm to R's right shoulder. To do this he turns his waist about his vertical axis. Ideally speaking, he is not pushing at all. R is pushing himself, through L.

A similar principle is used in the revolving doors of a hotel entrance. You push one "shoulder" of the door, it revolves around its vertical axis, and the other "arm" or "shoulder" moves back towards you. The door has no force of its own, it is like the famous fighting cockerel referred to in *The T'ai Chi Workbook*. It is all *your* force.

So if you try to approach your study of Push Hands along the lines suggested in this brief chapter, reducing the human body to points, lines, curves, and forces of pushing, yielding, and transmission, you will discover new things. In actual practice, of course, the play of emotions and tensions will influence the theories you pose yourself, but this is part of the enjoyment and interest of Push Hands.

10 *The Shape of the Movement*

What is an ugly movement? Is any movement intrinsically ugly? Or is it more a matter of association, in which we see something that reminds us of an event or feeling we don't like and then describe the movement as ugly when in fact it is the memory that is ugly? It seems likely that both are true. *Ugly, beautiful, pleasing,* and amusing are all words we can use to describe movement, and we can ask the same question about each description. The shape of the movement and the tone or manner in which it is performed both need to be taken into consideration. In T'ai Chi the tone of movement should be calm and slow. The shape is curved or even completely circular. Sometimes the curves are large, as in Diagonal Flying and sometimes very small, as in the wrist action of Single Whip—as big as the horizon or as small as a hairpin curve.

My own thoughts about this are connected with music. We rarely like music that goes on and on with no recurring theme. For some reason we all appreciate music that has one or more themes recurring in different parts of the piece, be it a symphony or a short, popular tune. Or the recurring section might be a rhythmic one. The musical passages may develop, they may be improvised on as in the case of jazz or Indian classical ragas, but there is a circular element. In the realm of movement, I believe, the curved or circular movement has a similar pleasing effect on both performer and viewer.

Everything in nature has a cyclic element, a kind of built-in predictability. When we perform T'ai Chi well we approach this natural cyclic world and step out of the jagged movement of modern life. If this is what we want on a daily basis, the study of the shape of our movement is important. In Push Hands the aesthetic aspect plays a much smaller part than in the Solo Form. Curves are seen as a practical necessity, first and foremost to enable us to yield. At the same time the experience

92

of yielding does itself depend on curves and circles, so that although the external movement may be less pleasing both to experience and to watch, the inner experience of yielding successfully can be doubly pleasing.

In photo 106 L begins to yield away in a curve to his left. In photo 107 he has come back to the center, and in 108 his whole trunk and leg are in a curved line taking his partner up off the ground. In photo 109 L has come up in a curve, ending in a Ward Off that sends L up and back. In photo 110 we are seeing a much closer contact where R has succeeded in bringing L's arm up to his body. L can move his body weight back and down, as he is beginning to do in photo 111, thereby causing R to extend his arms almost to the full. Alternatively, he can sit down and back, leaving space between body and arm (photo 112), or turn to his right (photo 113). In all cases he is using the curved yielding.

While the symphony of curves and circles is being rehearsed and performed in all its variety and cyclic nature, there is something that is con-

106

107

108

109

110

111

stant. In music it may be the key or the tempo. In T'ai Chi it is the vertical axis of the body (the spine) and its partner (the center of gravity). Together they play a kind of constant duet, keeping the curves and circles from going too far, like a musical key signature. If the body leans too much and the center of gravity goes too far, there is loss of balance, discord. However far and however fast the body may have to move through space, we try to keep a constant vertical and a low center of gravity. This can be done only through having a kind of uniform muscle tone combined with a readiness to move in any direction, whether pushed or pulled. We can use the phrase often used to describe systems in nature, *dynamic equilibrium*. Although superficially the two words may seem to be contradictory, a closer examination shows that they are not. A flat rock can be said to be in a state of equilibrium, but it cannot adapt itself to an earth tremor or landslide. It will be moved and will stay wherever it falls or slips. There is no dynamic element to rectify the changes. A T'ai Chi student begins from a state of equilibrium and is pushed. Uniform muscle tone and a *response* to the push enable the student to maintain the vertical axis and not be pushed off balance. This equilibrium is dynamic.

112   113

As an interesting example of this we can take a movement that reminds us of the internal martial art of Pakua, or Eight Trigrams. This requires several foot-turning movements and a 360-degree turn about the vertical. Suppose your partner pushes you on the outside of the right shoulder (photo 114) taking you forward initially. In response you begin to turn out, with the left foot. You regain your vertical position, continuing to step round (photos 115–118). Note that the hands are raised. The left is coming round at shoulder height and the right at hip

114

115

116

117

118

height. The reason for this hand position is clear in photo 119 where you have completed the circle and are beginning to push your partner's hip and shoulder (photo 120). Notice that you have slightly lost the vertical in photo 119, but this is compensated for by pressure on the sole of the left foot. Your partner is being sent backwards. Once again, the distance between the two men has been exaggerated for clearer viewing. A variation is shown in photo 121, where you are stepping in to drive your palm under your partner's left arm. If you train at this spinning type of technique you will experience the complete turning through 360-degrees and need to trust your legs to bring you to the right position to push your partner. It is an all or nothing experience. If you hold back or try to think about it, you will falter and fail. Once you have confidence in this technique, vary it by letting your partner push your right shoulder, as usual, but then push your left shoulder before you complete your turn, so that you have to turn back towards your original position. It is important in this exercise to turn the head and look where you are going, immediately. Do not wait until the last moment, as this may cause you to lose your balance from the sudden jerk of the head. Also, with your head turned you can see where you are going.

119   120

Keep the idea of the vertical with you all through your training. Keep with it the idea of a low center of gravity. This applies to the body as a whole but also to the parts. As an example take the Ward Off Left position of the left arm. All too often one sees the upper arm held horizontally, with the left shoulder unnecessarily raised. This wrong position upsets the center of gravity through some complicated network of muscular tensions. It is as though several extra pounds of weight have been added to the left arm, making it upset the balance and making the person vulnerable to a push there. The shape of the movement has been disturbed, and the consequences follow.

There are various other mistakes indicated by the shape of the movement. In photo 122 L has stepped into trouble, but R is also making a mistake. R is pushing but his legs are too far apart and he cannot really complete his push. L is beginning to step back with his right foot to take the push. In photo 123 R has this time moved in close; his arms are well placed to push but still his feet are too far apart and he is going to have to rely on his arms to complete his push. His legs are out of the action. In photo 124 L is raising his right foot to step and yield back and to his left rear diagonal direction to receive the push from R's arms.

122   123

If R were now pulled along his center line, he would have no chance of recovery (photo 125).

Photo 126 shows a bundle of mistakes. L has attempted Shoulder Stroke. But he has stepped in with such a big stride that he cannot bring his rear leg up. His left foot is not in a position to give a stable base, and his head is turned away from his partner. R has given way to his left and can easily pull L backwards or push him forwards. In photo 127, L has made the opposite mistake. He is too close. His front foot is in so deep and his center of gravity is so unsupported that R has only to press down on him to make him sit down quite forcibly. His rear heel is raised, giving him no base except for the toe, and this is too weak to counter his fundamentally wrong positioning.

These photographs show lack of cohesion between the different parts of the body. It is a broken shape. One part is going ahead of or lagging behind the others. In Push Hands when one part moves, everything moves. Then the center of gravity will be in the right place.

To concentrate more on your shape, train at the Push Hands movements alone, as well as with a partner. When you practice the push, as you step forward, bring the rear leg up into position at once. Do not leave it dragging behind you. An alternative is to bring the rear leg up closer to the front leg before you step and push, so that the completed position will be the standard one and the rear leg will not be left behind. Train, too, at spinning, by turning the toes in and out. If you spin to your left, turn the left toe out and the right toe in until you complete the circle. One of the purposes of turning the rear toe in is to give a stronger push from the rear foot as you turn, carrying you further round with one step.

Conclusions

There is sufficient material in this book to enable you to travel a long way in Push Hands. If you experiment and think about what you are doing, you will discover hundreds if not thousands of variations. You will see links with other martial arts without having to go and study them. In my opinion, Pakua and to a lesser extent Hsing-I—the two other internal Chinese martial arts—can be discovered from the principles of T'ai Chi. One of the reasons I never studied Pakua myself was that I did not want to learn just more and more techniques but to try and explore the working of a principle. The principle applies to all techniques; the techniques are simply examples of the principles.

125

126   127

11 Taoism and T'ai Chi Ch'uan

Author's Note: As many of my readers and students know, I am not in favor of forced breathing exercises of any kind, nor the unguided manipulation of the energies of the human body. So this chapter should be read merely as one explanation of Taoist ideas and practices and not as some kind of minimanual for would be practitioners of Taoist self-development.

I can sincerely use the traditional Eastern expressions of self-depreciation and self-effacement and say that this chapter is my own miserable and unworthy contribution to a subject that has produced mountains of books on its elusive yet ever-fascinating nature. I console myself with the *Tao-te Ching*, the written core of Taoism, traditionally ascribed to the sage Lao-tse. Arthur Waley commented that of the fourteen hundred translations of the book, "none plumb to the heart of Lao-tse." If at least such a number of experts could not, then how can I? Cheng Man-ch'ing took Waley to task over this and said that he had "gall" to write such a thing. This was presumably because no translation can plumb the heart of Lao-tse and it does not need an English scholar to say so! Lao-tse himself wrote, "My words are very easy to understand." Cheng said, "How is it, then, that even after more than a thousand expert commentaries, we are still in suspense?" Unlike Waley, Cheng does not condemn translators for failing to do the impossible. He merely raises the question of suspense.

My starting and finishing point is just that. We are still in suspense, we will continue to be in suspense, and we are meant to be in suspense. One may say that the *Tao-te Ching* is a work of concentrated wisdom that can be understood slowly, like water seeping through rocks or that can be understood when, at moments, one has flashes of insight from a deeper level of oneself. This bifocal approach to the book is approved of by many scholars and students of Taoism, who describe the two ways as a way of wisdom, or accumulation, and a way of insight, or intuition. Such a book does not belong to any particular period of history.

It is above social and cultural contexts. Its message is beyond the grasp of time and place.

The word *Tao* means a Way or a Path. The oldest pictorial record of the word is found on oracle bones and depicts a leader and a follower both treading the same path. Although *Tao* has been used by other traditions in China—such as the Buddhist—it really belongs to prehistory. No one knows when the Way began in China. The Tao, or Way, is presented as a kind of omnipresent, intelligent force or energy that gives and preserves life. The follower of the Way is one who has found the way of harmonizing himself with this energy, letting it work through him; he lives in accordance with the Tao. The *Tao-te Ching* makes it plain that it cannot be defined in words, only experienced. T'ai Chi Ch'uan is a vestige of this great teaching. One may describe how to do T'ai Chi Forms, how to do Push Hands; but finally only each individual student can find for him- or herself how to let the energy flow, coordinate all the body, relax the brain, release the breathing, and receive that rare impression of being at one with everything. You may recall that it is called "meditation in movement."

Lao-tse disappeared suddenly from public view, leaving his book behind him. It was a signpost, something to say that a very unusual human being had been here, had gone hence; a man who had understood life very differently from most of us. Every time you read it, you may feel you are getting close to something different, which then seems to evaporate. You may experience similar things in doing T'ai Chi. Sometimes it seems that you are relaxing much more than usual, for a few seconds maybe, and then you are just your usual you. You are in a sense always in suspense, because you never know when this different experience will come, and you are not sure how it comes, nor whither or why it goes.

There are many clues to the mystery, though. These clues are related to the study and understanding of oneself. The *Tao-te Ching* implies a teaching that is found in the ancient Indian traditions. This teaching says that all the universe, all creation, consists of the same primal substance. The many manifestations of this substance, from the stars and planets down to the tiniest creature, are all produced from one. Because they are all produced from one, each can influence the other. It is only in the West that the artificial division between mind and body was so powerfully made. Mind and body, in the *Tao-te Ching* and in the Indian tradition, are simply different gradations of the same fundamental substance. This is our first clue. Our thoughts, emotions, feelings, sensations, and movements are all potentially related to one another. So a performance of the T'ai Chi Form depends very much on how I am, in every respect. If I am agitated or am turning over a problem in my mind, the body and its movements will reflect this condition. There is no escape from it. On the other hand, if I begin to do the Form, thinking furiously about something else, then the movement of the body can influence my thinking and calm it down. It is a two-way process that is possible. In doing the Form we try to be empty of thoughts and empty—or at least less full—of tensions, and in this condition we can receive something of the Tao. Lao-tse's words remind us of the Gospels when he says, "Be empty and you will be filled." In a similar vein there is much made in the Taoist teaching of the idea of losing. Cheng told people to "invest in loss," echoing Lao-Tse's "He who has only a little will receive." Loss of what? If we make common sense our starting point, we shall say, "loss of what we do not need: our unnecessary thoughts, our agitation and our tension." In this condition, if someone pushes me, so what? Why be agitated? Why resist? What is there to lose if I have already lost it?

Scholars believe that when the Indian Buddhist teaching came to China there was a kind of blending of the foreign way with what was best in the indigenous Taoist way. This blending gave rise to a third way, the Ch'an teaching. Ch'an Buddhism is a singularly Chinese approach to the Indian way, and it found root also in Japan, where it became known as Zen Buddhism. The sudden enlightenment, or *satori*, of zen is found in stories both of Taoist and Ch'an origin. Robert K. Douglas, professor of Chinese at King's College, London, wrote in 1889 that after the appearance of the *Tao-te Ching,* subsequent Taoist writings built an inverted pyramid. The top, as I see it, was the best, and was at the bottom; and the higher you got, the nearer you got to the bottom. This little paradox smacks of Lao-tse. Chuang-Tse, a spiritual descendant of Lao-Tse, should be seen in a more kindly light. Thomas Merton said of his works that in them we "discern clearly a dilution of the *Tao-te Ching,* but a dilution only in the sense of a blending of its wisdom with the happenings of daily life." Though the Japanese people accepted Zen and cultivated it in the same way that Chuang-tse cultivated Taoism, they neither absorbed nor produced anything akin to T'ai Chi, as far as I know. The Tea Ceremony, for instance, is not the same: it has its own virtues, but they are different. In modern times the Japanese have become keen T'ai Chi students, but, as so often happened in the past, they learned from the Chinese.

Merton's expression, "blending of its wisdom with the happenings of daily life," is another clue for us in approaching Taoism as T'ai Chi students. T'ai Chi need not remain an isolated exercise, however uplifting or soothing or enlightening. Its philosophy of Yin and Yang is too grand to be contained in a fragment of the day. It is said that the original idea of Yin and Yang expressed the shaded and sunlit parts of a landscape. In the agriculturally based communities of ancient China the use of nature to transmit an idea is understandable. Jesus used parables related to the lives of his listeners: sheep and shepherds, vineyards and seeds. However, the cultivators of the fields and the shepherds were not weighed down by the mountains of data of all kinds that clog up the nervous systems of twentieth-century men and women. Sunlit and shaded fields, lost sheep, and fig trees are not the materials we work with. We can look rather at the telephone and the television, the computer and the commuter train.

With a little imagination of a constructive kind we can try to emulate Chuang-Tse and mingle the Tao with our daily lives. Take once more the idea of Yin and Yang, soft and hard. This is sometimes referred to as "the opposites," such as long and short, outside and inside, and so forth. Taoist teaching says that we all tend to see things in terms of opposites, as for instance liking this person and not liking that one. But this is all relative. I may dislike my boss, but if he promotes me or gives me an extra week's holiday, I suddenly like him. But rarely do I see him as he is, neither liking nor disliking. For that, in a sense, I have to be empty. If empty, I can see, I can hear. A more concrete example is this page you are reading. It is small and it is large. It is small compared with a billboard advertisement downtown; it is large compared with the period at the end of this sentence. But it is also itself, compared with nothing else. Just this unique, one page. No comparisons but just seen, from an "empty" mind. This possibility is always present if we remember it.

Although Lao-tse is the most famous Taoist, he was not the first. Huang-Ti, the Yellow Emperor, predates him by about two thousand years, and his book, the *Nei Ching,* or *Classic of Internal Medicine,* similarly predates the Tao-te Ching. Huang-ti is said to have lived around 2,500 B.C. and Lao-tse around 500 B.C. No dates are conclusive. The *Nei Ching* illustrates the application of fundamental Taoist ideas to medical diagnosis and treatment, as well as healthy living. It takes the form of questions put by Huang-ti to the T'ien Shih, or Master of Heaven—a man holding the highest rank in the Taoist hierarchy—and the latter's replies. In book 1 the question is put, "I have heard that in ancient times the people lived to be over a hundred years, and yet they remained active and did not become decrepit in their activities. But nowadays people reach only half that age and yet become decrepit and failing. Is it because the world changes from generation to generation? Or is it that mankind is becoming negligent of the laws of nature?" Ch'i Po, the T'ien Shih, answered, "In ancient times those people who understood Tao [the way of self cultivation] patterned themselves upon the Yin and Yang [the two principles in nature] and they lived in harmony with the arts of divination." Speaking of the Taoist sages, he goes on, "their vital original spirit was preserved within; thus, how could illness come to them?"

Here we meet an idea that recurs in Taoist writings up to the present time: Longevity. This idea has expanded to mean a healthy old age, a search for an alchemical elixir of life, and a spiritual inner transformation. A healthy old age we can all understand; the other two ideas are not so easy. Yet modern teachers such as G. I. Gurdjieff have also referred to this question of immortality. In *Meetings with Remarkable Men* Gurdjieff's father says, "A man is born with a certain property and, thanks to this property, in the course of his life certain of his experiencings elaborate in him a certain substance, and from this substance there is gradually formed in him 'something or other' which can acquire a life almost independent of the physical body." Through certain inner exercises, which will be presented later, the Taoist teaching says that this "something" can be produced more quickly and lead towards immortality of a kind.

The lessons of the *Nei Ching*, besides forming part of Taoist thought for forty-five hundred years, continued to support the development of Chinese medicine for an equal period of time. Though the ancient Greek Hippocratic oath has continued to provide an ethical basis for Western medicine to the present day, the writings of Huang-ti provided the Chinese with a permanently valid practical one. Herbology, moxibustion, massage, acupuncture, town planning, building and decorating, government, all sides of life in China owe much to Taoist ideas expressed in the *Nei Ching*. In the West we still search for synthesis, but without a root. Fundamental to T'ai Chi is the idea of being rooted, of having the weight down, of being supported from below. In the West we are not just in suspense, the suspense is killing us. We have lost our roots. We have lost touch with the Tao. This is a further clue.

The Man of Tao is rooted in something. It must be akin to Jesus' parable of building upon rock and not upon sand. T'ai Chi illustrates this in a simple, physical way. It is not my resistance, my pride, or my imagination—all built on sand—that will help me but the acceptance of Yin and Yang. The parable of the rock and the sand made one definite point—about durability. It did not speak of change as such. The title of the other magnificent Taoist classic—*I Ching*—means *"Book of Changes."* Accepting Yin and Yang means to accept change, change that accommodates the Tao. It also points to not jumping ahead to change before it comes and not being sure that a particular change will come. I can illustrate this from my own childhood.

Cars did not travel so fast in those days and the journey to London took nearly a whole day. I could not wait to get there and would ask my father, "When will we get there?" He would reply, "Round the next bend." When we rounded the next bend we would still not be there, and he would inevitably reply, "Round the next bend." Of course it was always the next. When my father was home on leave from the Royal Air Force in the Second World War and we went out for a walk, I liked to hold his hand. He would hold out his hand, and then as I grasped it he would fold it shut so that I could not. A real Taoist.

So the Tao holds us in suspense. We read and read, waiting for the final line in a long, funny story. We *could* enjoy the story even though we know the end will come. But is it just round the next bend or two-hundred miles away? When we push hands, are we waiting for the defeat or victory or are we experiencing? Defeat and victory are extremes of Yin and Yang, but experiencing is just being there, seeing, sensing and listening. Living. In his book *The Way of Chuang Tze*, Thomas Merton quoted a marvelous passage:

The goal of fasting [of the heart] is inner unity.
This means hearing, but not with the ear;
Hearing, but not with the understanding;
Hearing with the spirit, with your whole being. . . .
. . . Hence it demands emptiness of all the faculties.
And when the faculties are empty, then the whole being listens. . . .
Look at this window: it is nothing but a hole in the wall,
But because of it the whole room is full of light.
Being full of light it becomes an influence
By which others are secretly transformed.

This section about words and ideas is very inadequate. It may leave you in suspense.

Tantalos was a figure in Greek mythology who, as a punishment, was obliged to stand on the edge of a lake but was unable to quench his thirst. Fruit trees proffered their food from above him, but he could not stay his hunger with it. The Tao is tantalizing but not so cruel. In T'ai Chi we have something to satisfy us, if only in part. But one may well ask what other methods Taoism offers? In the West today we have thousands of books about how to change, how to be wise, happy, fulfilled, and so forth. We have thousands of people telling hundreds of thousands—if not millions—of others that they have the answer. Many of the tellers need to be told. To be fair, there is an incredible richness in this literary outpouring, mainly from East to West. The difficulty is in discriminating. In the face of a vegetable diet, a macrobiotic diet, a water cure, a bee sting cure, a Yoga course, a Rolfing course, an acupressure treatment, an aromatherapy treatment, a Zen meditation course, a Taoist meditation course, a Transcendental Meditation course, a Tibetan Buddhist course, a Sufi course, a music therapy course, a Shinto initiation, a biofeedback treatment, an encounter group, a mystical Christian retreat, and so on and on, what is the man or woman to decide? One of the most insidious aspects of this situation is that many groups offering help claim that their way is the only one. The now-enlightened readers of this book, having understood something of the Tao, can boldly assert that no system encompasses the Tao and therefore that this claim is manifestly false. While one system may not have everything, to embrace them all is just like simultaneously standing on your head for twelve hours, chewing all your brown rice two hundred times, bringing your *prana* out of the end of your big toe nail, chanting to the rhythm of your colonic contractions, holding your breath for ten hours, smiling at your neighbor and thinking positively, deciding water is good for you, and working out what is the sound of one hand clapping—clearly an effort beyond you and me.

There are without doubt sincere and informed teachers in the world, compassionately trying to transmit ways of understanding. I know some and possibly you do too. But there are also charlatans, get-rich-quick merchants, and simply misguided people. As my own life has partly cast me in the role of someone giving advice in this area, I feel that I must share what I can about it before going on to speak about the traditional Taoist methods, presented in our time in what I believe is an incomplete and therefore dangerous form.

Our Western education conditions us, like computers, to believe that we can change things just by wishing to do so. We find that something is "wrong," either with ourselves or our surroundings, and, unlike the Taoists, we immediately think, How can I change it? I seems to me that to change we first need a different understanding of the situation. It is like pushing. When I first hear of Push Hands training, I may think that I should resist and stop the push. First I need to find out what the situation is. So first I must have some new knowledge. I must know about how I function as a human being with thought, feelings, and a body. If something is wrong with my car, I must know how it is before I can repair it. This change that books and teachers speak of does not begin with taking on board a completed set of beliefs and practices nor with believing the untested words of a guru who may have some kind of authority over you. Because our spiritual life is at a low ebb, those of us who seek something are very vulnerable. We want someone to show us the Way but in the words of Lao-tse we should "be cautious, like one crossing a stream." Do not stand on the first stepping stone just because someone puts it down in front of you. This may be our first salutary step on the path of suspense: to seek but wait. It is a kind of discipline, to seek and wait. It needs a kind of honesty with one-self. It has been said that at one time we had faith, a deep faith, like the early Christians. But this seems to have almost disappeared, so we cannot rely on it. We cannot trust the inherent wisdom of the body, as we are no longer aware of it as the most ancient of human beings are said to have been. What we once had we no longer have. What remains is our capacity to know, to find out, to try.

In this connection we need to use a basic human potential that has still not vanished completely: honesty. I mean not that you should not fiddle income tax or not use the office telephone for private calls but that you should be honest with yourself. If we return to Push Hands, we can test our honesty easily. I do some pushing and yield to my part-ner, but suddenly I find that in spite of the fact that ten seconds ago I could yield and told myself I would continue to yield I am now resist-ing. I am the same person, it seems, but now I have changed. How can this be? This observation—just this—is more important than a thou-sand courses on self-perfection, because I made it myself. It is my own, unaided, and honest perception. I am still trying to be honest with myself and use my brains. I think to myself, "I decided to yield and I did, but now I—the same person—suddenly resisted without want-ing to." How can this be? What does it mean? How is it to be understood? I cannot remember. This is important. I cannot remember what I had decided. I decided to yield and then I resisted. It was the same person, Paul Crompton, and he did two opposite things.

You may find this quite unremarkable or you may wonder about it. If you wonder about it you may care to realize that it brings something quite new: it brings me new knowledge about myself. We see a film about war or starvation, and we know something, something with a different weight from knowing a telephone number or the time of day. This new knowledge belongs in a different place because it has a different quality. It brings up questions, it brings up doubts. It brings new life. This is our new Taoism, our new Zen. It shows us that discrimination, largely conceived as an intellectual function, is closely related to honesty, the functioning of which has an emotional element. If we remember the idea that everything in the universe consists of gradations of the same fundamental substance, we can see that this idea helps to explain the interplay of thinking and feeling in ourselves. Honesty and discrimination influence one another. If you find that the existence of two contradictory impulses in yourself—yielding and resisting—is a startling discovery, you will feel concerned. Not worried, but concerned to find out more. So honesty and discrimination have led to another experience—concern. We use different words to describe these different inner processes because in fact they consist of different substances. The importance of this will become clearer when we look at Taoist methods.

When we discover something new, such as the facts that I have tried to clarify above, we usually want to go out and tell someone else about it or at least talk about it to ourselves. It is as though we cannot bear to keep this discovery inside. We want to let it out. This new substance begins to wake me up about my situation, but I want to let it out and go back to sleep. Bearing in mind that this is a new substance, I can reason with myself that my desire to get rid of it is partly to be explained by the fact that there is at present no substance in me that can blend with the new one. But if, for instance, I could feel grateful—if another substance, gratitude, were to appear in me—perhaps the new experience, the new discovery, could blend with that. You may have seen, in pictures of Eastern temples, guardian figures at the entrances. These figures, often shown in strong, firm attitudes or postures, represent substances or possibilities in a man or woman; guardians, as it were, of new, enlightening experiences; guardians of awakening.

With these guardians present, the thieves of new experience cannot sneak in.

In my own discussions with a few self-professed Taoists and in all the reading I have done, I have never found anything similar to the approach I have tried to outline above. What I have tried to say is that before we undertake change we have to undertake discovery. Discovery about ourselves is related to the process of purification spoken of earlier. What follows is a short description of what modern Taoist teaching says one should begin with. It is building on sand. It is building the second floor of a house before the walls are up or the foundations laid.

Traditional Taoist teaching as presented today recognizes that there are many different substances in man and in the outside world. There are "six kinds of air," three substances to make the elixir of immortality—*ching* (essence), *ch'i* (breath), and *shen* (spirit)—and many lesser agencies or substances to assist the transformation of these primary substances. *Ching* is the sperm of the male body, but it also has a finer, or manifesting, energy, which gives the body its vitality. *Ch'i* is not only the actual breath, or air, that a person breathes but also the energy of the universe, which also gives a vitality. *Shen* is described as a spiritual consciousness that existed before a man was born. This provides another form of vitality. The idea is that by the adept's transforming the *ching* the *c'hi* becomes transformed and then by further elaboration the *shen* is transformed. These three sequential processes produce the elixir. The elixir of immortality is the goal of Taoist teaching. Its production depends on Taoist ideas on meditative breathing, correct posture, and inner silence. The transformed substances follow a definite route through the body. They proceed through various vital points, or *chakras* (as defined in Yoga), passing down the front of the body and up through the tip of the spine up to the crown of the head.

During this process, the student will often experience heat, may be subject to illusions of many kinds caused by the circulation of energy, and may also experience congestion of energy at any of the vital points through which the energy passes. These include the tip of spine, the sexual region, the navel, the solar plexus region, the base of the throat, the point between the eyes, and the crown of the head.

Several modern commentators on this process have related it to the electrical activity of the nervous system. They say that the constant and repeated concentration by the student on this circulation of energy produces a change from positive to negative on the outside of the nerve fibers. There is a buildup of potential within the student and this can from time to time produce a big release of energy along the nerves. The nervous system is depolarized, and an experience of clarity, or enlightenment, is possible. It is understandable to be concerned about the release of energy itself, the "thunder and lightning." What is aimed at is the calm after the storm.

Taoists who approach T'ai Chi purely from a meditative viewpoint regard the exercises as a help in stimulating the transforming flow of energy. That is why the subject of breath control appears with such regularity in books on the subject. It is claimed that the movements of the Form are related to different points in the circulation of the energy and that if the Form is done correctly, with right breathing, it will assist the sitting, meditative training. A glance at an elementary book on physiology will show that the glands and organs of the body are connected to the sympathetic nervous system, and the slowing and deepening of the breathing plays a vital role in this effect. In stories and accounts of Taoist students' experiences there is usually a teacher involved who is able to give some guidance. There is no mention made of any preparatory period in which the student cleared the ground for what was to come. If we think about this and acknowledge that the Taoist Way is an authentic Way both in its own right and as an accepted source for the appearance of Ch'an Buddhism, this missing preparation must have been part of the training. What should strike us as we read Taoist and Ch'an and Zen accounts of a students' experiences is that the students themselves were exceptional men. Because they are described as students we tend to think of them as if they had just walked in off the street. We see a gulf between the student and the teacher, but we do not see the gulf between the student and the man in the street. There is in fact a big difference. It may be that the difference between the man in the street and the student is bigger than the difference between the student and the teacher.

The circulation of energy round the body, passing through vital centers, is, as it were, the high road, the superhighway. So where are the side roads, the back streets? Learner drivers do not learn on the superhighway or freeway. So even in this "pedestrian" analogy there is a lesson for us. Before driving on the superhighway we have to learn on the side roads and back streets. In terms of T'ai Chi Push Hands this brings us back to our basic difficulties. The panorama in Push Hands of tensions, resistance, oppression, pride, and ambition to succeed momentarily mirrors the even greater panorama of difficulties that faces us in approaching the Way of Taoism. Before we can proceed to the main highway of the grand circulation of energy we must steer our way through the minor roads of our own imperfections. Until you can find a teacher who can show you how to do this, it is better to leave the main highway alone.

Coming back to the *Tao-te Ching*, there is a great deal within its pages that can vivify and enrich our study of Push Hands. The book says that the Tao is inexhaustible. The quest to do Push Hands perfectly is also virtually inexhaustible. However much we try to follow the Yin and Yang we shall perhaps always fall down, either by yielding too much or pushing too much. In each case we shall lose our equilibrium. But the possibility of trying again does not disappear, and it is this possibility that makes Push Hands inexhaustible. It is not in the success that we find our fulfillment but in the gift of being able to try again.

It is also said that the Tao cannot be expressed. Right Push Hands cannot be expressed either. It is rather an experience, requiring a constant and unwavering attention so that neither Yin nor Yang—yielding nor pushing—becomes more important than the other. It is a teaching and a lesson without words. Ambition and the desire to succeed are out of place here. Ambition ties one down and leads to blindness to what is taking place. Instead of being able to follow what is taking place we are led to try to make things happen when ambition is leading us. Instead we should wait to be moved, follow, add strength when we have to, and give up strength when necessary.

The *Tao-te Ching* says that there is no contention, no battle, and no blame. In Push Hands we try to forget ego and harmonize with what is taking place. We do not impose our *selves* on what is happening. If I fall, it is not my partner's fault. It is my fault for resisting or yielding too much. So I do not blame my partner. Nor do I really blame myself. I can begin again.

I try to become soft and pliant like a child, another expression from this classic book. I follow the ebb and flow of things, letting my breath move naturally, at peace with my surroundings. There is "no chasing, no hunting, not striving, not forcing." I try to become watchful, like an open window. I am cautious, "like someone about to cross a stream," yielding to my partner, "like ice that is about to melt." As the temperature and pressure varies so do my Yin and Yang. I am watchful and obedient. My partner does not notice my existence, I am so attuned to him.

When the Tao is present and manifest, there is a constant, dynamic equilibrium of pushing and yielding, Yin and Yang. When the Tao is lost, "out come all the differences between things." When the Tao is lost, out come all the differences of contention and ambition, hunting and chasing, resisting and forcing. So we restrain our ego and "curtail our desires."

Can there be competition when there is no one to compete? In Push Hands we do not compete, so no one can compete with us. Likewise, no one is rejected, because there is no opposition. He who insists loses the Tao. We do not insist on pushing so we do not lose. When cooking a small fish, says the *Tao-te Ching*, we do it gently or it will be destroyed. When we do Push Hands, we do it gently or equilibrium will be lost. We "deal with a thing before it comes into existence," detecting Yang before it overcomes us. In Push Hands we do not know what to do, so we know best.

Conclusion

As Taoism might itself say, Push Hands is a mountain, a molehill, and itself. If we look at all the difficulties at once, it is a mountain. If we regard it beside all the difficulties of daily life, it is a molehill. If we simply deal with it as it comes, it is itself.

Like the cherished notes of a favorite piece of music, the familiar experience of working with a partner for mutual benefit and understanding may be anticipated as one of the oases of life. To step outside the pushes and pulls of life into a world of direct and immediate experience whose consequences harm no one is a relief. When it can lead to a better understanding of that world outside, it is much more than a relief. It opens up a new world. The new values to be found in miniature in the Push Hands "playground" point towards the new values we all need to find in this century. Push Hands is an education. Perhaps it is part of that education we have not received as children. I wish you good luck and hope you "graduate."

Some Taoist Terms

In Taoist thought the approach to understanding and enlightenment touched on in this book belongs to the method called *ching*. This involves meditation, exercises, quiet sitting, and closer acquaintance with breathing. The approach that uses thinking, studying, reasoning, and question-and-answer is known as *ming*. Ideally speaking both the *ching* and *ming* would be combined in understanding the Tao.

The word *te* is used to describe the experience of enlightenment. The Zen Buddhists have the word *satori* and the Hindus the word *samadhi*.

In trying to establish the inner circulation of energy, the Taoists unite the energies of the heart and kidneys, or *k'an* and *li*. The heart is also referred to as the dragon or the sun, and the kidneys as the tiger or the moon. The union of the sun and moon produces the internal circulation.

The spot below the navel is referred to as the *ch'i-hai* or, more popularly, *tan t'ien* and is regarded as the most important center, particularly for men. The breathing in and out used to stimulate the inner current is known as the bellows, or *t'o yo*.

Just as in the T'ai Chi Form the four cardinal points of the compass are used to decide direction of movement, the inner circulation passes through four major points of north, or *tzu*, which is the root of the penis; south, or *wu*, which is the top of the head; east or *mao*, on the back; and west, or *yu*, in the front.

The best-known circulation channel is the microcosmic orbit, or *hsiao chou tien*, which begins at the base of the spine, rises to the crown, and descends down the front of the body through the different vital centers. Almost every book in print that mentions it gives this direction. In one work, however, this is described as a Yang, or stimulating, current, but the opposite direction of circulation is given as a calming, or Yin, current. My own guess is that this second, opposite direction is one of the missing parts of present Taoist teachings.

Saliva is regarded by Taoists as a vital source of energy and is sometimes called Golden Nectar. In T'ai Chi some teachers tell students to rest the tongue at the root of the upper teeth to increase the flow of saliva. Swallowing the saliva slowly is said to aid the circulation of energy.

In Chinese tradition the number five is very important. In medical theory the five elements should be balanced to maintain health. By cultivating them the Taoist aims to produce the elixir of immortality. Five organs in the body are related in the effort to stimulate the circulation of energy. These are the kidneys, or water element; the heart, or fire element; the liver, or wood element; the lungs, or metal element; and the spleen, or earth element.

The human being in general is always looking outside himself for satisfaction. In Taoist terms this loss of vital energy is harmful to the aim of immortality. To preserve the spirit, or vital energy, the Taoist tries to practice *chu chi*, or storing up of vitality.

The idea of fire is very important in Taoism. Eighteen different kinds of fire are referred to. This is a Yang force and moves energy from different vital points in the body. In spite of being a Yang force, fire is sometimes said to have a quieting, or shrinking, or Yin, action. This seems to be a contradiction and I have not yet understood it.

You may have seen pictures of the Buddha lying down on his side. This posture is used by Taoist and Zen students to preserve energy while resting. The head rests on one palm, whilst the other palm lies across the abdomen. One leg is almost straight and the other is bent. It is sometimes called Coiling the Body into Five Dragons. I have not come across an explanation of the action of the posture itself.

In T'ai Chi writings one sometimes reads expressions that seem totally incomprehensible. For years I read the words "breathing through the heels." What did it mean? I guessed various things till I came across the following. In the oldest archeological pottery figures one finds monks sitting not cross-legged as in Indian tradition but sitting back on the heels, that is, kneeling down with the buttocks resting more or less on the heels. The proposition is that this more ancient method of sitting involved bringing the energy round the body and "breathing" through the lowest part, which is the part in contact with the heels. To breathe through the heels may therefore not refer to an action carried out while doing T'ai Chi but while doing seated meditation.

In T'ai Chi the upward and downward presentation of the palms represents an alternation of Yin and Yang positions. But the right hand itself is Yang, and the left hand Yin. They are known as the Lair (or Opening) of the Dragon and the Tiger.

Students of Zen know that one of the methods of approaching enlightenment is the process of question-and-answer between student and teacher, called *mondo* in Japanese. It attempts to bypass the intellect of the student in favor of direct perception. In the Taoist tradition a similar method is used, called *wen ta*. For example Chuang-tse described the point of *wen ta*: "To ask questions which cannot be answered is the way of a fool. To try to answer questions for which there is no answer shows a lack of understanding."

Another Zen method is known as *kung an* or *koan*. A student comes to the teacher and asks a question to which the teacher answers, "Have some tea." Another student comes with a different question and the teacher answers, "Have some tea." The first student asks the teacher why he gave the same answer to a different question, and the teacher replies, "Have some tea." If the student's mind is ready, he will suddenly understand something from the fact that the answer is not rationally related to his question, though in another sense it is.

Ch'uan shen means to show forth the spirit. It is used in connection with something a student produces, such as a painting or a poem. In the most highly prized work there is something of the artist or poet himself in the brush strokes. In both Chinese and Japanese painting the breathing of the artist plays an important role and experts claim they can "see" the breath in the painting, showing forth the spirit of the artist.

These are a few of the hundreds of terms used in Taoist and T'ai Chi theory. Unfortunately there is no universal agreement of terminology or on methodology today. Many volumes would be needed to present all the variations.

Bibliography

Blyth, Reginald H. *From the Upanishads to Hui-neng*. Vol. 1 of *Zen and Zen Classics*. Tokyo: Hokuseido, 1960.

Cheng Man-ch'ing [Cheng Man-jan]. *Lao-tze, "My Words Are Very Easy to Understand": Lectures on the Tao Teh Ching*. Trans. Tam C. Gibbs. Richmond, Calif. North Atlantic, 1981.

_____ and Robert W. Smith. *T'ai-Chi: The "Supreme Ultimate" Exercise for Health*. Rutland, Vt.: Tuttle, 1971.

Crompton, Paul. *The T'ai Chi Workbook*. Boston: Shambhala, 1987. Also published as *Chinese Soft Exercise*. London: Unwin, 1986.

Da Liu. *The Tao of Health and Longevity*. London: Routledge & Kegan Paul, 1979. New York: Schocken, 1978.

De Bary, William Theodore; Wing-tsit Chan; and Burton Watson, eds. *Sources of Chinese Tradition*. Vol. 1. New York: Columbia University Press, 1960.

Douglas, Sir Robert K. *Confucianism and Taouism*. London: Society for Promoting Christian Knowledge, 1889. New York: E. & J. B. Young, 1889.

Gurdjieff, Georges I. *Meetings with Remarkable Men*. Trans. A. R. Orage. London: Routledge & Kegan Paul, 1963. New York: Dutton, 1969.

Lao-tzu. *Tao Te Ching*. Trans. Ch'u Ta-kao. London: Unwin, 1976. New York: Weiser, 1973.

Lü Tung-pin. *The Secret of the Golden Flower*. Trans. from Richard Wilhelm's German by Cary F. Baynes. Routledge & Kegan Paul, 1962. New York: Causeway, 1975.

Merton, Thomas. *The Way of Chuang-tze*. London: G. Allen & Unwin, 1970. New York: New Directions, 1965.

Smith, Robert W. *Chinese Boxing: Masters and Methods*. New York: Kodansha, 1974.

Waley, Arthur. *The Way and Its Power: A Study of the Tao and Its Place in Chinese Thought*. London: Allen & Unwin, 1968. New York: Grove Press, 1958.

The Yellow Emperor's Classic of Internal Medicine. Trans. Ilza Veith. Berkeley: University of California Press, 1972.